The Middle East in Crisis

Books from
FOREIGN AFFAIRS

America and the World: Debating the New Shape of International Politics *(2002)*

The Clash of Civilizations? The Debate (1996)

How Did This Happen? Terrorism and the New War
Edited by James F. Hoge, Jr. and Gideon Rose *(2001) PublicAffairs*

The American Encounter:
The United States and the Making of the Modern World
Edited by James F. Hoge, Jr. and Fareed Zakaria *(1997) BasicBooks*

FOREIGN AFFAIRS
Editors' Choice

Globalization: Challenge and Opportunity *(2002)*

The Middle East in Crisis *(2002)*

The Rise of China *(2002)*

The War on Terror *(2002)*

Closing the Great Divide: Development and the Eradication of Poverty *(2001)*

Intervention and American Foreign Policy *(2001)*

The New Terrorism *(2001)*

The New Trade Agenda *(2001)*

The United States and the Persian Gulf *(2001)*

The United States and Russia *(2001)*

Weapons of Mass Destruction: Threat and Response *(2001)*

Foreign Affairs Agenda: The New Shape of World Politics *(1999)*

Is Global Capitalism Working? *(1999)*

Competitiveness: An International Economics Reader (1994)

For additional information visit
www.foreignaffairs.org/reader/reader.html

FOREIGN AFFAIRS EDITORS' CHOICE

The Middle East in Crisis

A Council on Foreign Relations Book

FOREIGN AFFAIRS

NEW YORK

Distributed by
W.W. Norton and Company
500 Fifth Avenue
New York, New York 10110

Founded in 1921, the Council on Foreign Relations is a nonpartisan
membership organization, research center, and publisher. It is dedicated to increasing
America's understanding of the world and contributing ideas to U.S. foreign policy.
The Council accomplishes this mainly by promoting constructive discussions and by publishing
Foreign Affairs, the leading journal on global issues. The Council is host to the widest possible
range of views, but an advocate of none, though its research fellows and Independent Task Forces
do take policy stands. From time to time, books and reports written by members of the Council's
research staff or others are published as a "Council on Foreign Relations Book."

**The Council takes no institutional position on policy issues and has no
affiliation with the U.S. government. All statements of fact and expressions of
opinion contained in all its publications are the sole responsibility of the author or authors.**

The Council's bimonthly magazine, *Foreign Affairs,* has been America's leading publication on
international affairs and foreign policy for 80 years. With a circulation of 115,000 worldwide,
Foreign Affairs has long been the most influential forum for important new ideas, analysis, and
debate on significant global issues. To subscribe, or for more information, visit
www.foreignaffairs.org.

Foreign Affairs books are distributed by W.W. Norton & Company (www.wwnorton.com).

Contents

From Peace to War

The United States and the Middle East

Introduction

Gideon Rose

WHAT A DIFFERENCE a few years can make. In the late 1990s, things seemed to be going fairly well for the United States in the Middle East. The peace process between Israel and its Arab neighbors was inching forward, Iraq remained under international quarantine, reformers were gaining ground in Iran, and Osama bin Laden was holed up in a remote Afghan hideaway. To be sure, pessimists had ample grounds for seeing the glass as half-empty: there was more process than peace, the international community was getting tired of containing Iraq, the Iranian reformers had powerful opponents, and every couple of years brought another terrorist attack somewhere linked to anti-American Islamist radicals. But considering the catastrophes that had marked previous eras and the scale of the region's problems, American policymakers surveying the scene had legitimate grounds for satisfaction and even hope.

Then the roof fell in. The Syrian track of the peace process was derailed in the spring of 2000, when a Geneva summit between President Bill Clinton and ailing Syrian leader Hafiz al-Assad ended in failure. The Palestinian track met a similar fate some months later. Over the summer, a Camp David summit between Clinton, Israeli Prime Minister Ehud Barak, and Palestinian leader Yasir Arafat failed to produce a deal, and in the fall a new Palestinian intifada erupted. The replacement of Barak by Ariel Sharon and Clinton by George W. Bush at the start of 2001 brought to power governments less interested in negotiations than their predecessors had been, while renewed Palestinian

GIDEON ROSE is Managing Editor of *Foreign Affairs*.

terrorism killed hundreds of Israeli civilians and eventually prompted an Israeli reoccupation of the West Bank.

In Iraq, meanwhile, Saddam Hussein began to extricate himself from the "box" in which the United States had tried to keep him confined. UN weapons inspections ended, sanctions were increasingly ignored, and Iraq's diplomatic isolation began to erode. Moreover, in Iran it became clear that President Muhammad Khatami and his band of reformers were stymied by an old guard determined to resist liberalization, and that no significant changes in Iranian politics or policy were likely in the immediate future. And then came September 11, 2001.

The attacks on the World Trade Center and the Pentagon had several consequences for American policy. Suddenly terrorism rose from being a tragic nuisance to the number one item on the national security agenda. The potential for a "clash of civilizations" between the United States and the Islamic world grew, as it became clear that the attackers were not fringe lunatics but the extreme wing of a movement that had disturbingly broad support in many Middle Eastern countries. The American relationship with Saudi Arabia came under increasing scrutiny because of the national origin of most of the attackers and the Saudi role in promoting radical Islamist ideology abroad. A lightning victory in Afghanistan left the United States with the difficult job of overseeing that nation's postwar political and economic reconstruction, even as operations in pursuit of escaped senior al Qaeda and Taliban leaders continued. And all the while the situation in Israel continued to deteriorate and the storm clouds gathered over Iraq.

In fact, as U.S. relations with China and Russia improved in the wake of the attacks, the various Middle East crises became the dominant items on the American foreign policy agenda. This collection offers a searching look at those crises, providing the background and perspective needed to understand the challenges they present and to think clearly about what tackling them will involve. Originally published in Foreign Affairs, the essays chronicle the collapse of the Middle East peace process and the course of the second intifada, the war on terror, and U.S. policy toward the Persian Gulf and other Mideast hotspots. Together they bring the reader up to speed on the dizzying events of the last few years in the region and offer a unique basis for informed discussion of where to go from here.

Introduction

THE END OF THE AFFAIR

THE SCENE on the White House lawn on September 13, 1993, marked a turning point in the history of the Middle East. The signing by Israeli and Palestinian leaders of the Declaration of Principles on Interim Self-Government Arrangements—also known as the Oslo Accords, for the Norwegian city where they were secretly negotiated in the previous months—seemed to pave the way for the end of the Arab-Israeli conflict, with the parties moving gingerly towards mutual acceptance as land and sovereignty were gradually traded for peace and security.

In spite of lingering suspicions and repeated setbacks, unprecedented cooperation between the two communities emerged during the remainder of the decade. Yet the hoped-for virtuous circle of mutual concessions, increased trust, and further concessions never materialized, and eventually the peace process collapsed into the tragic bloodshed of the second intifada. Why Oslo failed and whether such failure was inevitable remain hotly disputed, whereas what will happen next and what role the United States can and should play remains unclear.

David Makovsky leads off the collection by describing the rise and fall of the Oslo process, carefully weighing the responsibility of all parties for what happened. He argues that some form of separation has become a prerequisite for resuming talks about the terms of the ultimate divorce, and suggests modest steps for how to protect and advance the progress achieved in recent years.

Khalil Shikaki, meanwhile, looks at the political dynamics of the Palestinian community before and during the second intifada. He sees the uprising as neither a plot by Arafat to weaken Israel and force it to accept extreme Palestinian demands, nor as a spontaneous response to Israeli provocations by an enraged but disorganized Palestinian "street." Instead, he argues, it has been a response by a "young guard" in the Palestinian nationalist movement to both Israeli actions and the failure of Arafat's "old guard" to deliver Palestinian independence and good governance.

Aluf Benn provides a complementary survey of the political dynamics on the Israeli side of the conflict, tracing the course of the

Sharon administration's first year in office. He argues that there was indeed a plan behind Sharon's policies, but one few want to acknowledge—an attempt to freeze the status quo.

Hussein Agha and Robert Malley pick up where Makovsky leaves off, writing an obituary for Oslo's incremental approach to peace negotiations and arguing for a dramatic external intervention that would present to the local actors the outlines of a sensible, comprehensive deal. "The point now should not be to accommodate the Israeli and Palestinian leaders' limitations and shape the effort to fit their proclivities; it should instead be to make the limitations of both sets of leaders irrelevant."

And Gal Luft, finally, builds on Shikaki and explores the rapid embrace of suicide bombing as a central strategy in the Palestinian national struggle as the "young guard" gains increasing influence. Palestinians know full well what they suffer at the hands of the Israeli military in response to such attacks, he notes chillingly, but support them nonetheless because they derive comfort and satisfaction from the fact that Jews are now suffering as well.

PAX AMERICANA IN PRACTICE

THE SEPTEMBER 11 ATTACKS at once epitomized and catalyzed the danger to the United States emerging from the Middle Eastern cauldron. Rather than coming out of nowhere, Fouad Ajami notes, the attacks emerged from a distinct regional context, one that needs to be understood in order to grasp both their true motivations and the later course of the war on terror. Arguing that on that day "the American imperium in the Arab-Muslim world hatched a monster," he shows how "terror shadowed the American presence in the Middle East throughout the 1990s" and how the attacks were but the latest episode in a relationship that had been troubled ever since the Persian Gulf War.

The mastermind of the plot, Osama bin Laden, was the son of a Saudi construction magnate and had supported the Afghan mujahideen in their struggle against Soviet occupation. Developing a vast network and organizing a series of deadly attacks on U.S. installations around the world, he sought to oust Americans from the Middle East, overthrow so-called moderate Arab governments, and create a unified Muslim nation based on a puritanically oppressive theology. Bin Laden saw the 1991 war against Iraq, the stationing of U.S. troops in Saudi Arabia, and American support of Israel as just the latest episodes in a long history of Western humiliations of the Muslim world. Media coverage of Palestinians hurt or killed during clashes with Israeli soldiers, meanwhile, fanned the rage of his followers and of Arabs and Muslims more generally—many of whom found bin Laden's radicalism appealing as a response to the poverty, frustration, and repression of their daily lives.

Martin Indyk observes that these feelings had been allowed to fester thanks to a bargain the United States had made with such countries as Saudi Arabia and Egypt during the 1990s:

Moderate Arab states would provide the U.S. military with access to bases and facilities to help contain the "rogues" and would support Washington's efforts to resolve the Arab-Israeli conflict; in return, Washington would not exert significant pressure for domestic change.

Indyk explains why this approach seemed like a good idea at the time, but why a different tactic may be appropriate now. "The United States will have to persuade the Egyptian and Saudi governments," he argues, "to address more effectively their people's basic requirements for greater political and economic progress."

Eric Rouleau probes more deeply into the current situation in Saudi Arabia and finds a country in trouble. Despite the efforts of reformers in the royal family, he notes, the kingdom is struggling with economic problems, social unrest, and popular outrage over the Israeli-Palestinian conflict. Radical Islam and anti-Americanism continue to simmer and could soon reach a dangerous boil.

Kenneth Pollack, in turn, glances ahead to Iraq, which many believe will be the next major battleground. Hawks are right to be concerned about the prospect of an unconstrained Saddam Hussein, he argues, but their critics are right in pointing out that the problem is not really related to September 11 and cannot be solved on the cheap. Finding all the alternatives to be even worse on close inspection, Pollack concludes that an invasion of Iraq designed to topple Saddam and replace his regime with something better is the route to take—but it should be approached as a second Gulf War, not a second Afghan campaign.

Puneet Talwar explores the stalemated U.S.-Iranian relationship in a piece written just before the attacks. He shows how Iran's conservatives, anxious to turn back a string of victories by Khatami and his reformist allies, embarked in early 2000 on a campaign of bloody repression that continues to this day. As the two camps battle for control of the Islamic Republic, he contends, the proper moves from Washington might be enough to tip the balance. He recommends a course of moderate engagement in order to help Iran's moderates help themselves—although the Bush administration, unconvinced by such arguments, is turning toward a harder line instead.

Continuing the survey of American relations with Middle Eastern troublemakers, Ray Takeyh notes that the conclusion of the trial of two Libyans for the 1988 bombing of Pan Am flight 103 over Lockerbie, Scotland, raised an interesting dilemma: What should Washington do when American containment policy starts to pay off and a "rogue" state starts to reform? After years of international isolation, Takeyh explains, Libya's Muammar al-Qaddafi is ending his belligerence and starting to meet many of the demands placed on him by Washington and its allies. The challenge for the Bush administration is to figure out a way to keep the pressure on while recognizing Libya's progress and helping reintegrate it into the world community.

The last two pieces in the collection, finally, move beyond country-specific analysis to treat the fortunes of the Islamist movement more generally. Graham Fuller notes that Washington's mantra that the war on terrorism is not a war on Islam ignores the reality that religion and politics are inextricably linked throughout the Muslim world. Rather than push secularism, he argues, the West should help empower the silent Muslim majority that rejects radicalism and violence. The result could be political systems both truly Islamist and truly democratic. James Piscatori, meanwhile, reviewing two major new studies of Muslim politics, finds Bernard Lewis tracing the Islamic world's problems back centuries and Gilles Kepel arguing that Islamism's moment has already passed. The struggle over who speaks for Islam, he concludes, is far from over.

Introduction

PLUS ÇA CHANGE

AT THE END of the Persian Gulf War in 1991, few would have believed that a decade later the situation would remain frozen, with Saddam Hussein still in power yet still on probation. It was similarly farfetched to imagine that the Israeli-Palestinian conflict would come full circle, moving from strife to harmony back to strife. And certainly no one would have predicted that a dozen years after the Soviets left Afghanistan the Americans would enter, achieving the kind of military success that the Soviets could only dream of yet not knowing what to do with the country once they had conquered it.

As the old saw runs, prediction is difficult, especially about the future. Yet it is hard to believe that given the fragility of the current situation, the strategic landscape of the Middle East and U.S. policy toward the region will not change dramatically once again, and in very short order. The catalyst could be an American invasion of Iraq, or a domestic upheaval in a crucial country, or an Arab-Israeli explosion (or breakthrough). Whatever happens, these essays should provide an indispensable guide for the perplexed.☯

From Peace to War

Middle East Peace Through Partition

David Makovsky

THINGS FALL APART

JUST LAST SUMMER, the seven-year-old Israeli-Palestinian peace process seemed on the verge of success. Palestinian Authority (PA) Chairman Yasir Arafat and Israeli Prime Minister Ehud Barak met with President Bill Clinton at Camp David and came close to agreement. But Arafat walked away from a deal at the last moment, and less than three months later the Occupied Territories erupted in violence. Now, after months of bloodshed and with the death toll approaching 400, it has become fashionable to say that the Oslo process (so called for the city where talks first began) is dead. Rumors of its demise, however, have been exaggerated. Its central objective—transforming the existential Israeli-Palestinian conflict by ending Israel's mutually harmful control over three mil-lion Palestinians in the West Bank and Gaza—remains as crucial today as it was seven years ago.

It was in Oslo in 1993 that the Israeli government, under then Prime Minister Yitzhak Rabin, first agreed to withdraw from parts of the West Bank and Gaza and opted definitively for territorial partition. With this shift in Israeli policy, Rabin crushed the Israeli

DAVID MAKOVSKY is Senior Fellow at the Washington Institute for Near East Policy and a contributing editor for *U.S. News and World Report*. A former executive editor of *The Jerusalem Post* and a former diplomatic correspondent for the Israeli newspaper *Ha'aretz*, he is the author of *Making Peace with the PLO: The Rabin Government's Road to the Oslo Accord.*

right's dream of a Greater Israel. And he signaled his support for a solution to the conflict that envisioned a new state of Palestine arising alongside an Israel finally accepted by the Arabs.

The peacemakers at Oslo foresaw both separation and cooperation for the two states. Partition would occur in stages and be facilitated by confidence-building measures and a gradual easing of Israeli-Palestinian enmity. The two sides would cooperate in such areas as security and trade and defer resolving the most divisive issues, including Jerusalem and refugees. Arafat took the helm in Gaza and the PA was established in 1994, but underlying grievances endured and the spirit of cooperation soon soured, leaving part of the Oslo vision unfulfilled.

Now the ongoing misery in the region has made it clear that partition remains the only feasible option for resolving the conflict. And as Israel's only hope for peace, partition should be pursued whether or not the Palestinians agree to it. After the disastrous past several months, something more modest than Oslo is now in order. The move to a comprehensive deal should begin with a less ambitious but still enormous step: disengagement, which would put as much space as possible between the two sides.

A key premise of the Oslo talks was that formal peace agreements would produce greater trust and security for both sides. But although several interim accords have been negotiated, such trust has shown few signs of developing. Disengagement now could jump-start the process and ultimately evolve into full state-to-state cooperation. Even if it does not, however, it is a practical approach that could achieve stability—the next best thing. Focusing on disengagement may mean that Oslo's promise of full cooperation remains unfulfilled for the moment, but the alternatives—occupation, ethnic cleansing (or "transfer," as it is called in Israel), and Shimon Peres' vision of a harmonious "New Middle East"—are either unworkable or unthinkable.

In his final days in office, Clinton put forward the most detailed peace plan of any American president to date. But the Clinton plan was unrealistic, since it assumed that the Israeli-Palestinian conflict was on the brink of resolution. Now President George W. Bush must push for something less grandiose than a comprehensive deal while trying to halt the slide toward a Kosovo on the Jordan or even a full-scale regional war.

Pursuing a middle course toward disengagement and then waiting for matters to stabilize should not, however, obscure the fact that Israeli-Palestinian cooperation remains a vital long-term goal. Just as current passions necessitate disengagement in the short term, the stubborn constraints of Middle Eastern geography necessitate cooperation in the long run. Israel has no military solution to Palestinian nationalism, and the Palestinians can never eliminate Israel through force. The two sides must learn to live together. After all, Israel at its center is no wider than Manhattan is long, and the adjoining West Bank is the size of Delaware. Israelis and Palestinians do not have the luxury of the kind of cold peace that Israel and Egypt—separated by hundreds of miles of desert—now share. Oslo's underlying two-state vision therefore remains sound, even as Israelis and Palestinians sift through the wreckage. Sooner or later, they will have to come back to partition.

WHAT WENT WRONG?

OUTSIDERS OFTEN ASSUME that the main source of conflict between the Israelis and the Palestinians is how to deal with the West Bank and Gaza. In fact, the conflict runs far deeper. Palestinians and Israelis have radically different historical narratives. These predate the occupation that began in 1967; they go to each side's self-conception as a historical victim, and they have engendered much mutual hatred.

Notwithstanding these deep grievances, however, Oslo suffered from more immediate problems: what the Palestinians failed to do, what the Israelis failed to do, both sides' unfulfilled hopes for the new PA, and the lack of strategy for final-status talks.

Perhaps Oslo's greatest problem was the inadequacy of the Palestinian leadership. Only Arafat—who embodied his people's nationalist aspirations since becoming leader of the Palestine Liberation Organization (PLO) in the late 1960s—had sufficient stature to sign an accord with the Israelis in 1993. But Arafat subsequently made three unprincipled decisions that crippled the peace process. First, he failed to repudiate violence as a negotiating tactic; in fact, he relished using it to achieve political goals. Second, Arafat subjected security cooperation with Israel to the vicissitudes of the political environment, thereby undermining Israel's faith in the stability of the "land for peace" equation. And third, unlike Nelson Mandela in South Africa, Arafat refused to equate peace with reconciliation, thus gutting any hopes that a deal between governments could be transformed into a far more meaningful—and lasting—peace between peoples.

The Oslo framework was based on Arafat's promise to Rabin that henceforth all disputes would be solved peacefully. To this end, Israel helped create an armed PA, giving it the security apparatus the Palestinian leaders deemed essential to wage war against the Islamist extremists of Hamas.

This Palestinian security force ultimately exceeded its agreed-on size limit by half and comprised no fewer than 12 different security services. Nonetheless, during the first three years of the PA's existence, Arafat resisted unceasing U.S. and Israeli entreaties to use his new muscle to clamp down on Hamas. According to the human rights group B'tzelem, 172 Israelis were killed during this period. All the while, Arafat gave speeches hailing the principle of jihad, and after the Hamas bomb-maker Yahya Ayyash was killed by the Israelis, Arafat publicly eulogized him as a martyr.

In 1996, when violence again erupted—this time after Likud Prime Minister Binyamin Netanyahu opened an underground tunnel near the plateau in Jerusalem's Old City that Jews venerate as the Temple Mount and Muslims as the Noble Sanctuary—Arafat remained silent for days before intervening to stop the riots, which killed 65 Palestinians and 15 Israelis. The rioting proved an effective bargaining tool for Arafat, breaking a logjam in negotiations then underway over Hebron. When riots broke out again on May 15 last year to mourn the anniversary of the birth of Israel and to demand the release of more Palestinian prisoners, precedent prevailed: Israel opted for diplomatic concessions once more, agreeing to yield villages around Jerusalem to PA control.

The most glaring example of Arafat's use of violence as a negotiating tactic came after last summer's Camp David summit. Arafat

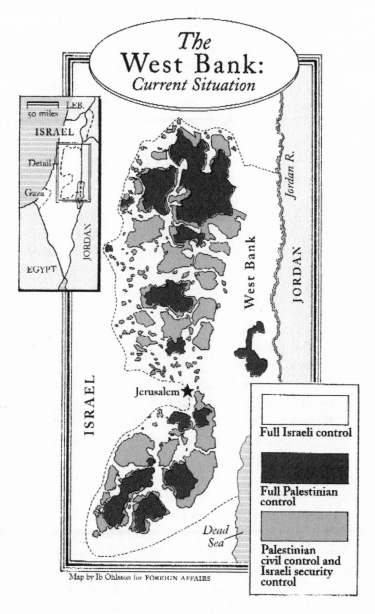

The West Bank: Current Situation

LEB.
50 miles
ISRAEL
Detail
Gaza
EGYPT
JORDAN

Jordan R.

West Bank

JORDAN

ISRAEL

Jerusalem ★

Dead
Sea

Full Israeli control

Full Palestinian control

Palestinian civil control and Israeli security control

Map by Ib Ohlsson for FOREIGN AFFAIRS

was unhappy with the American and Israeli positions—which included an offer of 94 percent of the West Bank and all of Gaza—but made no proposals of his own. Whether or not he was actually responsible for the subsequent outbreak of violence remains subject to debate. But there can be little doubt that he fueled the fighting instead of trying to stop it. State-run Palestinian media exhorted crowds to participate, and daily coordinating meetings took place between Arafat's Fatah movement and members of Hamas and Islamic Jihad. On two separate occasions in October, the PA released known terrorists from prison, which seemed to be a green light from the PA for the subsequent terror attacks. Despite making promises to Clinton and other top U.S. officials, Arafat took near-ly two full months to issue his first call for the Palestinians to reduce (but not halt) the bloodshed.

In a similar vein, the PA has often refused to coordinate security measures with Israel over the years. Security cooperation—which was to be Israel's principal benefit from Oslo—was held hostage to politics. As Israel's Deputy Defense Minister Ephraim Sneh put it in the fall of 2000, "the Palestinians have not delivered on Oslo's basic bargain: [a] state for security." This utter refusal of PA security forces to maintain direct contacts with the Israelis—or even to answer their cell phones during times of tension—eventually com-pelled the Clinton administration to use the CIA to help fill the void by acting as a liason between the two sides.

Beyond the use of violence as a negotiating tool and the on-again, off-again nature of security cooperation, Arafat's third failure of leadership was his refusal to publicly chart a course for reconcil-iation. After all, "land for peace" had been the original premise of all Arab-Israeli negotiations. Oslo was structured around step-by-step withdrawals and based on the implicit belief that further Israeli land concessions would take the edge off Arab enmity, which in turn would ease Israeli opposition to a Palestinian state. But as land was handed over, Palestinian calls for reconciliation never came. No programs were ever implemented to this end; in seven years, Arafat never gave a single speech in Arabic to his own people calling for reconciliation. This failure was critical, for arguments over the per-manence and legitimacy of a Jewish homeland in the Middle East remain at the very heart of the Arab-Israeli conflict.

Arafat's failure to bury the hatchet has been duly noted by his constituents—as a comprehensive poll taken by the Ramallah-based Bir Zeit University last November showed. When asked whether they would recognize Israeli sovereignty over West Jerusalem if Palestinians gained sovereignty over East Jerusalem, an overwhelming 74 percent of Palestinians said no. Furthermore, 60 percent said they did not think there was a chance for peaceful coexistence between Palestinians and Israel. Another Palestinian poll released in December found that a full two-thirds of Palestinians supported "suicide operations" against Israel. These numbers are not surprising. After all, Arafat himself has likened peace with Israel to the Treaty of Hudabiyya, the temporary truce that the Prophet Muhammad made with the non-Muslim Quraysh in 628 AD—only to conquer those same people years later. Such rhetoric has made peace with Israel sound like a short-term ruse. And such sentiments were further exacerbated when Arafat publicly expressed doubts about Jewish attachment to the land of Israel. Arafat further alleged that Israel was "forging its history and reality" by claiming the existence of two ancient Jewish temples in Jerusalem.

All the while, Palestinian state-run media and state-backed Islamist preachers in mosques have launched unrelenting, venomous attacks against Israel and Jews. Palestinian schoolchildren are often taught to hate from a young age. And they are prevented from learning anything about Israel; the Jewish state's existence and location are conspicuously absent from many of their textbooks.

By articulating support for coexistence, Arafat could have moderated Palestinian hatred and broadened the Israeli public's support for withdrawal from the Occupied Territories. Egyptian President Anwar al-Sadat's statesmanlike visit to Jerusalem in 1977 had just such an effect. Arafat's failure to take such steps left Israeli moderates politically vulnerable—especially Rabin, Barak, and Peres.

FACTS ON THE GROUND

ISRAEL'S RECORD is not flawless. It did keep its end of the core bargain with the Palestinians by letting Arafat return to Palestine, by enabling the establishment of a Palestinian proto-government, and by giving it land to govern. Although the Israelis may not have violated the letter of their agreements, however, they certainly broke their spirit in one particularly sensitive area: settlements in the West Bank and Gaza. During the original Oslo talks in 1993, the Palestinians had wanted an explicit Israeli commitment to a settlement freeze. But Rabin, leery of a confrontation with the settlers, refused. And Israel, under both Labor and Likud governments, supported ongoing Jewish settlement expansion.

According to Israel's dovish Peace Now, settlements today take up only 1.36 percent of the West Bank (excluding East Jerusalem and access roads), but the issue remains emotionally charged. Residential housing units under construction in the territories have expanded by 54 percent since 1993, and the number of Jewish settlers has grown from 115,000 to about 177,000. Bypass roads built to limit friction between settlers and Palestinians have only made things worse: Palestinians see the roads as land expropriations designed to make life easier for the settlers at Palestinian expense. As for the settlements themselves, most of the growth has taken place in three blocks near the pre-1967 borders of Israel, in areas that Israel intends to annex (the annexation was reportedly accepted by Arafat at Camp David). But the new homes—with their modern red-tiled roofs and community swimming pools—have created resentment among the Palestinians, who see them as an Israeli attempt to prejudice talks on final borders.

LETDOWNS

ON TOP OF Palestinian incitement and Israeli settlement expansion, each side feels the other has failed to observe its commitments under Oslo, thereby undermining faith in the integrity of the process.

Palestinians complain that Israel has repeatedly broken its deadlines for withdrawing from the West Bank. Although Israel has in fact yielded 40 percent of the West Bank to full or partial PA control, and although virtually all Palestinians now live in such areas, the Israeli occupation has been only partially dismantled. Signs of Israel's ongoing control abound, and these—especially the Israeli checkpoints on main roads between Palestinian cities—are offensive to Palestinians.

Israel, meanwhile, complains that the PA releases Hamas terrorists from its custody in a revolving-door fashion, that weapons are regularly smuggled into the territories, and that the agreed-on quotas of the number of Palestinian security forces have been blithely ignored. When the Netanyahu government shone a spotlight on the fact that Palestinian textbooks and state-run media continue to challenge Israel's very existence—in violation of Oslo provisions against incitement—the prime minister was derided for seeking a pretext to halt the peace process. But the Israeli left could never explain why, if the PA was genuinely committed to partition and coexistence, it refused to stem the tide of bilge.

In addition to these grievances, the PA itself represents an enormous economic and political failure. In the six years following Oslo, the Palestinians saw their per capita GNP remain flat at $1,600. The Palestinians blame this on Israel's tight control of their borders and its closures of the territories during much of this period. Until a wave of Palestinian knifings of Israelis in early 1993, an estimated 140,000 Palestinians worked as day laborers in Israel, either legally or illegally, and they made vital contributions to the underdeveloped Palestinian economy. But the number of day laborers plummeted in the aftermath of terror attacks, and they were eventually replaced, mainly by Romanian and Thai guest workers. The majority of Palestinians, including Arafat, decried the closures as collective punishment, souring the climate still further.

Despite Palestinians' complaints, however, many of their economic woes are self-inflicted. Arafat has done little to wean his people from their economic dependence on Israel. The PA's only notable economic success was the creation of a casino in Jericho, which attracted Israelis forbidden to gamble inside Israel's borders. As a revolutionary, Arafat has considered it beneath his dignity to focus his energy and resources on economic development; last summer he angrily waved away CNN reporter Christiane Amanpour when she asked him about such issues.

As bad as they are, the Palestinians' economic woes are only part of a broader problem: namely, scant government accountability. The PA is thoroughly corrupt. And although it has a popularly elected legislature, its executive branch remains authoritarian. Israel, which believes that a strong-armed government is more ruthless and hence more effective at fighting terror, has not pressed for reform. Thus the Palestinian rulers, insulated from the public, have managed to shirk responsibility for their misrule and blame their problems on external foes.

A SLOW ROAD TO NOWHERE

THE GRADUALISM that was Oslo's signature style held both promise and peril. Unfortunately, instead of slowly building support, the incremental Oslo process let leaders on both sides defer tough decisions on core issues. This delay wound up eroding confidence rather than enhancing it. The process also allowed each side to make contrary claims at home. With no road map for a final deal, Israeli leaders were able to continually promise their constituents what they wanted—including a united Jerusalem under Israeli sovereignty—while Arafat could promise his people what they wanted—including the right of return for all Palestinians to long-abandoned homes inside Israel. Arafat sold Oslo to his public by telling them it guaranteed a return to the 1967 lines and entailed no compromises. He led his people to believe that they would get 100 percent of the land they wanted. This unsurprisingly led to unrealistic expectations and the explosion of frustration (egged on by the PA) that followed the failure of Camp David.

When it finally came time to discuss the ultimate issues, still another set of problems arose. Barak came to office in the summer of 1999 promising to solve the entire Arab-Israeli conflict within a year. This pledge was based on his willingness to make far-reaching concessions, on his excellent relationship with Clinton, and on his desire to counteract the threat posed by the rising power of Iran and Iraq. Barak figured that his best chance to get the Palestinians to compromise while neutralizing the last military threat on Israel's borders was to cut a separate deal with Syria. But when the Syrian track collapsed in the spring of 2000, it proved to have been a major detour, consuming the first eight months of the Barak administration—the time when the premier's popularity was at its height.

By spending so much time on the Syrians, Barak more than halved the period in which he could strike a deal with the Palestinians and still reach the September 13, 2000, target date for the end of negotiations. Then, to make matters worse, after details from secret talks in Stockholm leaked last summer, the Palestinians refused to discuss issues seriously. Meanwhile, the United States failed to persuade either Egypt or Saudi Arabia to acquiesce to a deal or provide sorely needed political cover for Arafat that would let him make compromises on Jerusalem. With the deadline looming, the Palestinians publicly complained that Israel was dragging its feet. But it was Barak who felt the keenest sense of urgency. Once the extent of his planned concessions leaked, his coalition effectively disintegrated, shrinking to 42 seats in the 120-member Knesset.

At the Camp David talks, both sides considered taboo-breaking concessions on once intractable issues. But the talks ultimately foundered on the questions of Jerusalem—specifically, Arafat's unwillingness to share sovereignty over the Temple Mount—and the Palestinian refugees.

Arafat never told the truth to the Palestinian exiles who fled or were chased from Israel in 1948: that not even Israel's leading doves could accept their return to the country. To allow three million Palestinians to return to a nation of five million Jews and one million Israeli Arabs would be the death knell of the Jewish state. Arafat should have told the refugees to focus on finding new homes elsewhere or next door, in the new state of Palestine. But he lacked the courage to do so. This made compromise all the more difficult.

THE ENDURING PROMISE OF PEACE

DESPITE its apparent failure, the Oslo process achieved many important gains for both sides, which should be kept in mind when discussing any future peace plan. The Palestinians won a peculiar country-like status, with institutions (including various ministries, a parliament, and security services) that would constitute the nucleus of their future state. And Arafat began to be treated everywhere as a de facto head of state. Before Oslo, he was not permitted to visit the United States; afterwards, he became the leader most often invited to the Oval Office. Clinton himself addressed the Palestine National Council in Gaza, which Palestinians saw as an endorsement of their hopes for statehood.

David Makovsky

For Israel, the gains came in different arenas. When security cooperation with the Palestinians actually worked, it had positive results. For example, in 1999 Israel suffered the fewest civilian fatalities due to terrorism (two) in any one year since 1987. Oslo also enabled Israel to transform its covert security links with Jordan into a full peace treaty and to strengthen its ties with strategically positioned Turkey. In addition, Israel gained lesser forms of diplomatic relations with 8 of 22 members of the Arab League. It participated in four U.S.-backed regional economic conferences, and Western investors poured billions of dollars into the country. Most important, the 1990s was the first decade since Israel's creation in 1948 that passed without an Arab-Israeli war.

OVER HERE

THE AMERICAN ROLE in the Israeli-Palestinian negotiations has varied over the last decade, depending on who held power in Israel. When the right-leaning Likud ruled, Washington took an active stance, fearing that a less conciliatory Israeli government might provoke a regional conflagration and jeopardize U.S. interests. Such activism led to the U.S.-brokered Madrid conference in 1991 and Wye River agreement in 1998.

When a center-left Labor government has led Israel, however, the United States has generally acted as a facilitator, helping out when needed but letting Israel set the pace. It is no coincidence that the original Oslo agreement itself was struck without U.S. involvement.

Washington dropped this back-seat approach last summer, however, when despite the constant dialogue, Israelis and Palestinians seemed unable to agree on final status issues. Led by Clinton, American diplomats at Camp David shuttled between the two sides; Barak and Arafat did not once meet alone during the 12-day summit.

It has become popular to blame Clinton for his intensive role at Camp David, but such critiques are unfair. Oslo and subsequent agreements had set target dates for resolving final-status issues, and these were about to expire. Moreover, Barak's ruling coalition was disintegrating. He himself asked Clinton to convene the summit, telling him the time was "now or never."

Clinton has also been taken to task for the last-ditch suggestions he made on December 23rd of last year. The lame-duck president presented the Israelis and the Palestinians with the most explicit and far-reaching proposals suggested by any American government to date. Under his plan, the Palestinians would get control of almost all of East Jerusalem, including much of the Old City; exclusive sovereignty over the Temple Mount; and a formula that would enable some Palestinian refugees—as determined by the Israeli government—to move into pre-1967 Israel. Barak provisionally supported the proposals, while Arafat's aides gave them "qualified acceptance"—with so many objections that the Palestinian acceptance was all but meaningless.

This time, the criticism of Clinton was merited. Although the U.S. president's proposals approximated the ultimate compromises necessary for a final deal, they were divorced from current reality. In the months since Camp David, the situation had changed drastically. Although sharp Israeli concessions might have been appropriate last summer, they were much less so after all the bloodshed. The latest uprising shattered hopes that the conflict would soon be resolved. And without an end to the fight in sight, the Israeli public now fears that far-reaching sacrifices on Jerusalem (of the kind Clinton proposed) will make them physically vulnerable. They are thus much less interested in compromise. Instead of pushing for a deal, then, the Americans should have focused on ending violence and restoring trust. In failing to do so, Clinton left a dangerous legacy for the new Bush administration; his ideas could become lasting U.S. policy whether or not an end to the conflict is within grasp.

BREAKING UP IS HARD TO DO

To UNDO the damage, Bush should now acknowledge that a comprehensive deal is not at hand, and he should work with Israel's new prime minister to enhance stability in the region while assuming that conflict may continue. Bush can do this by promoting disengagement. This would not close the door on a broader ultimate deal, however, for disengagement is an interim idea. But the length of this interim should not be set by an artificial deadline. Before moving toward closer ties, Israel should look for tangible signals that the Palestinians are truly ready to end the conflict and start cooperating. The criteria of cooperation are not amorphous. They include resolving disputes peacefully, guaranteeing permanent security cooperation, and working toward reconciliation. This last point means putting an end to the use of state-run media and school curricula to delegitimize Israel, and promoting instead a normalization of ties between the two societies. Until such criteria are met, diplomacy should be predicated not on the Oslo assumption of land for peace, but on something less romantic: a strategic Israeli withdrawal from most of the territories in return for a protracted truce or the kind of nonbelligerency that Israel and Egypt agreed to in 1975 (the "Sinai II" disengagement agreement), which paved the way to their 1979 peace treaty.

Such a middle path has advantages for both sides. Modern Israel cannot retain control over all its biblical territory while remaining a Jewish state and a democracy. And only after the Palestinians relinquish claims to the 1948 borders can they start addressing their own endemic problems.

If done properly, disengagement will provide Israel with more rational and defensible borders and give the Palestinians the potential for a viable state. Israel should consolidate its settlements in the West Bank into three blocks (where close to 80 percent of the settlers already live) while dismantling all of the other smaller and less defensible settlements elsewhere in the territories (including all the settlements in Gaza). Israel could then annex the consolidated West Bank settlement blocks as envisioned at Camp David. This would serve Palestinian interests as well. The Palestinians would still get the overwhelming majority of the West Bank and Gaza. And consolidation would make their territory contiguous, not split apart by scattered Israeli settlements and access roads. Meanwhile, keeping the populations apart and erecting borders between them would reduce the grinding friction that has poisoned relations over the last 33 years.

European Union–style open borders between the two states may be possible at some point in the future, but only after a drastic improvement in relations. Israelis today are justly afraid of terror-ism, and the Palestinians justly want the Israelis out of their lives. Polls demonstrate that disengagement is popular in both commu-nities. And if the violence worsens, disengagement will become even more attractive.

Of course, cooperation is ultimately necessary, for only by coop-erating can the two sides resolve the vital issues of refugees and control of Jerusalem. Deciding the status of the Jordan Valley—the eastern frontier where Iraq attacked Israel in 1948 and menaced it in 1967—may also have to be deferred until Israel finally makes peace with Iraq. But such cooperation can come only after disen-gagement, not before it. As Rabin once put it, Israelis and Palestinians should "separate out of respect."

Meanwhile, disengagement would allow the Palestinians to declare statehood, a cherished goal. Israel would be able to with-draw its troops. And disengagement would provide a psychological boost to both sides, who have been badly traumatized in the last generation. Palestinians have suffered the humiliating Israeli occu-pation, while Israelis have lived with the daily threat of terrorism. Each side now needs some breathing space to recuperate, and a border behind which to do so.

This does not mean that a Great Wall of China should be built in the Middle East, however. A wall with windows is required. The geography of the region is so intimate that the two states will have to share resources such as electricity grids and water for the foreseeable future. The PA depends on Israel for a third of its GNP, and if regulat-ed properly, economic interaction could continue. Furthermore, the two sides need to cooperate on security, as Israel does with Jordan.

Disengagement would preferably be achieved by agreement and not simply a unilateral Israeli fiat. Such an agreement might anger those Israelis who now believe that nothing can be gained from further negotiations with the truculent Palestinians. Unilateral action would also be tempting because it would enable Israel to draw its own territorial lines, regardless of the impact on the Palestinians. Such temptation should be resisted, however, unless the Palestinians refuse to cooperate and Israel is left with no alternative.

There are several reasons why a deal on disengagement—even a tacit arrangement—would be better than a series of uncoordinated, unilateral land-grabs. Due to the small size of the region and the need for a shared infrastructure, security cooperation, and economic links, any uncoordinated step is guaranteed to cause conflict. Second, coming on the heels of last spring's unilateral Israeli pullout from Lebanon, an unnegotiated withdrawal from the territories would further erode the perception of Israel's strength in the neighborhood. Indeed, Hamas has already trumpeted what it calls the "Hizbullah model" for gaining territory: do not negotiate with Israel—expel it. Many Arabs would therefore likely interpret the immediate, unilateral dismantling of several isolated settlements as a sign of Israeli weakness. On the other hand, a deal on withdrawal would give Israel the political cover needed to dismantle settlements without undermining its deterrent.

An agreement, then, is clearly preferable to unilateral Israeli action. If the Palestinians prove unwilling to comply, however, Israel should wait until the current violence dies down—or simply wait for a decent interval—and then act alone to disengage.

BUSH'S BURDEN

THE SCALED-DOWN approach to Middle East peace presented here should not seem alien to the Bush administration. After all, Republican realists traditionally argue that security emerges not from a contractual peace but from realistic, mutually acceptable arrangements designed to enhance stability.

To lay the groundwork for disengagement, the United States should help the Israelis and Palestinians contain the chaos and halt the violence. The Bush administration must discourage what PA cabinet minister Nabil Sha'ath has called the "Algerian model"—to negotiate amid violence. There should be no diplomatic reward for bloodshed. Secretary of State Colin Powell and other top aides should also recognize how the toxic public environment is poisoning negotiations and get serious about combating incitement. And they should be less tolerant of violations of the agreements by either side; peace will not work if treaties are not implemented fully and fairly.

At the same time, the United States should do what it can to make the PA more viable, encouraging Palestinian economic development in order to dilute the PA's dependence on Israel. Washington should urge the Persian Gulf states to use a fraction of their recent oil profits to employ Palestinians as guest workers. And the United States should start promoting Palestinian democracy in a bid for more accountable, less corrupt government.

Finally, Washington must remind the parties—both Arafat and Israel's newly elected prime minister—that merely creating a border will not absolve them of their responsibilities. Palestinians and Israelis must learn to speak the language of reconciliation, or else cooperation will remain elusive. Even once a real border and state-to-state relations are established, consistent joint counterterrorism efforts will remain essential.

Above all, the Bush team must understand that it cannot walk away from this volcanic situation. The stakes for Washington are high, and benign neglect of the Israeli-Palestinian conflict will occur at America's peril. More than at any other time in the last three decades, tensions in the region now have the potential to escalate. The situation could quickly change from a nationalist conflict to an absolutist religious struggle or from an isolated fight to a regional conflagration. Top American national security officials have called the Middle East the most dangerous flash point in the world. If Clinton was drawn to Middle East peacemaking by rising hopes, Bush will be dragged in by rising fears. The region remains of critical importance to the United States due to the U.S. dependence on affordable oil from the Persian Gulf, its desire to contain a defiant Saddam Hussein, and its special relationship with Israel.

Any American Middle East strategy should therefore include other countries in the region. Apart from Israel, the United States must also consult with its Arab allies, especially Egypt and Saudi Arabia. Although almost no Arab leader wants a war with Israel, one could still break out. The Hizbullah militia, for example, has sought to exploit the current violence by launching cross-border attacks from Lebanon, despite Israel's unilateral exit from that country. Washington has warned Hizbullah's

Syrian patrons that it will not restrain Israel from retaliating against Syria for further attacks, which could easily lead to war. Such an Israel-Syria clash could quickly spread. Indeed, there have already been massive public demonstrations in Arab capitals—especially Amman, Cairo, and Rabat—protesting the violence in the West Bank and Gaza. The situation could therefore rapidly spin out of control.

A SEPARATE PEACE

THE IDEA of partitioning the region first arose in 1937, when the United Kingdom, which then held the League of Nations Mandate for Palestine, set about to restore order after the Arab riots of the previous year. In its report on the violence, the Peel Commission wrote,

> An irrepressible conflict has arisen between two national communities within the narrow bounds of one small country. There is no common ground between them. Their national aspirations are incompatible. The Arabs desire to revive the traditions of the Arab golden age. The Jews desire to show what they can achieve when restored to the land in which the Jewish nation was born. Neither of the two national ideals permits of combination in the service of a single State. ... But while neither ... can fairly rule all of Palestine, each ... might justly rule part of it.

The idea of partition was accepted by the Jews then but fought tooth and nail by the Arabs. Only half a century later would the Palestinians finally come to accept the commission's logic. For all of Oslo's problems, the ideas of separation and mutual recognition remain its irreducible core and its most important legacy. Peace will come to the region only through partition—not because it is an ennobling or lofty vision, but because there is simply no other way.⊕

Palestinians Divided

Khalil Shikaki

WHO LET THE DOGS OF WAR OUT?

HAS YASIR ARAFAT, the president of the Palestinian Authority (PA), orchestrated and led the second Palestinian intifada in order to gain popularity and legitimacy while weakening Israel and forcing it to accept extreme Palestinian demands? Or has the uprising been a spontaneous response by an enraged but disorganized Palestinian "street" to Likud Party leader (and later Israeli Prime Minister) Ariel Sharon's September 2000 visit to the site known to Jews as the Temple Mount and to Muslims as al Haram al Sharif, and the failure of the Oslo peace process to produce an end to Israeli military occupation? Most Israelis take the first position, whereas most Palestinians take the second. Both are mistaken.

The truth is that the intifada that began in late September 2000 has been a response by a "young guard" in the Palestinian nationalist movement not only to Sharon's visit and the stalled peace process, but also to the failure of the "old guard" in the Palestine Liberation Organization (PLO) to deliver Palestinian independence and good governance. The young guard has turned to violence to get Israel to withdraw from the West Bank and the Gaza Strip unilaterally (as it withdrew from South Lebanon in May 2000) and simultaneously to weaken the Palestinian old guard and eventually displace it.

More than a year into the intifada, the young guard's commitment to both goals is unshakable, and with some reason. The Israelis have begun seriously to consider unilateral withdrawal, and the young

KHALIL SHIKAKI is Associate Professor of Political Science at Bir Zeit University and Director of the Palestinian Center for Policy and Survey Research in Ramallah.

guard has assumed de facto control over most PA civil institutions, penetrated PA security services, and forced Arafat to appease the newcomers for fear of losing his own legitimacy or bringing on a Palestinian civil war. In fact, at this point only the prospect of a truly viable peace process and a serious PA commitment to good governance can provide Israel and the old guard with an exit strategy for their current predicaments.

TREND SPOTTING

THE INTIFADA has crystallized two important trends within Palestinian politics and society. The first, a split between old and young guard within the nationalist movement, has greatly constrained the PA leadership's capacity to manage the current crisis and engage in substantive negotiations with Israel in the short term. The second, a broader decline in the power of the nationalists relative to the Islamists (such as Hamas), has created a long-term challenge to the nationalists' ability to lead the Palestinian people.

When the Oslo agreement was signed in September 1993, two-thirds of the Palestinian public immediately supported it.[1] Expectations were high: Oslo was supposed to usher in the end of occupation, the establishment of an open and democratic political system, and a quick improvement in economic and living conditions. But the golden era of the peace process did not last long. Palestinian popular approval of the Oslo process peaked at 80 percent in early 1996, and support for violence against Israeli targets bottomed out at 20 percent. Just before the Palestinian general elections in January of that year, support for Fatah, the mainstream nationalist movement headed by Arafat, reached the unprecedented level of 55 percent, and Arafat's own popularity leaped to 65 percent. Meanwhile, support for all

---

[1]The figures cited here are based on more than 75 surveys conducted by the author in the West Bank and the Gaza Strip, including Arab East Jerusalem, in 1993–2001. The sample size in each of the surveys ranged between 1,300 and 2,000 people in face-to-face interviews. Details about the survey methodology are available at the Web site of the Palestinian Center for Policy and Survey Research (http://www.pcpsr.org).

opposition groups combined—both nationalist and Islamist—dropped to 20 percent, down from 40 percent two years earlier.

When the current Palestinian political system came into existence after those elections, it had real legitimacy. Seventy-five percent of eligible voters participated, despite the call by opposition groups for a boycott. Arafat received more than 70 percent of the vote, with about 22 percent casting blank ballots and only 8 percent voting for his rival, Samiha Khalil. Fatah won 77 percent of the seats in the new Palestinian Legislative Council (PLC).

Between 1993 and 2001, with the sole exception of 1994, Palestinian support for the Oslo agreement never dropped below 60 percent. But Palestinian hopes began to fade as a result of both Binyamin Netanyahu's election as Israel's prime minister in mid-1996 and the continued building of Jewish settlements in the West Bank and the Gaza Strip. Palestinian expectations that the peace process would soon lead to statehood and a permanent settlement dropped from 44 percent during Shimon Peres' prime ministership in 1995–96 to 30 percent in the first year under Netanyahu. Four years later, with Ehud Barak having replaced Netanyahu and Jewish settlements continuing to expand, expectation of a permanent settlement sank to 24 percent. Once Ariel Sharon won election as Israel's head of government in early 2001, a mere 11 percent of Palestinians clung to that hope.

The loss of confidence in the ability of the peace process to deliver a permanent agreement on acceptable terms had a dramatic impact on the level of Palestinian support for violence against Israelis, including suicide bombings against civilians. In July 2000, after U.S. President Bill Clinton's failed attempt to broker a final peace settlement at Camp David but before the eruption of the second intifada, already 52 percent of Palestinians approved of the use of violence; a year later, that figure reached the unprecedented level of 86 percent. Other casualties of Oslo's demise have been the popularity of Arafat and that of his Fatah organization. The Camp David summit brought Arafat's popularity, which had been dropping steadily since 1996, down to 47 percent. A year later it hit 33 percent. Support for Fatah, meanwhile, dropped to 37 percent in July 2000, and a year later fell to 29 percent.

Surprisingly, before the intifada the Palestinian Islamists did not significantly benefit from Arafat and Fatah's decline—deserters from the mainstream nationalist cause simply chose to remain on the political sidelines, and the Islamists' support levels hovered consistently around the mid-teens. The intifada changed that dynamic, however. By July 2001, the Islamists' popularity had increased to 27 percent. And for the first time ever, support for Islamist and nationalist opposition groups combined, at 31 percent, surpassed the 30 percent garnered by Fatah and its allies.

The collapsing peace process and deteriorating economic and living conditions are not the only factors bleeding the ranks of Arafat and Fatah's supporters. The Palestinian public's evaluation of the status of Palestinian democracy, official corruption, and governmental performance have moved from bad to worse over the past six years. In 1996, 43 percent of those surveyed gave Palestinian democracy and human rights a good bill of health; by 2001, only 21 percent agreed. Over the same period, positive evaluations of the performance of PA institutions dropped from 64 percent to 40 percent, and the belief that the PA was corrupt increased from 49 percent to 83 percent.

The intifada has only aggravated the Palestinian public's disappointments. The unrelenting Israeli siege and closure of Palestinian territories, with the consequent debilitating restrictions on movement, have practically halted Palestinian civil, social, and economic life. In July 2000, fewer than one-third of Palestinians believed that violence would help achieve goals in ways that negotiations could not; a year later 59 percent had come to that conclusion. Indeed, after nine months of the intifada, 71 percent thought that the fighting had already had such an effect.

The perceived failure of the peace process, combined with a highly negative assessment of all issues related to PA governance, delivery of services, and leadership, damaged the legitimacy of the PA and the nationalist old guard it represents. It created an opportunity for other forces within the Palestinian community to step forward, and this is precisely what the younger generation of leaders did in the fall of 2000—taking advantage of Sharon's provocation and the subsequent turmoil to seize the moment and challenge their internal rivals.

WELCOME TO
MILITARY BOOKSTORE
SERVING THE BEST CUSTOMERS
IN THE WORLD.

MIDDLE EAST IN CRISIS
9780876093177   14.25

TOTAL $14.25
CASH $14.25

ITEMS 1
05-06-2004   09:03
6241 01 000001   5393

SAVE YOUR RECEIPT
FOR A QUICK REFUND
VISIT US AT
WWW.AAFES.COM

CHANGING OF THE GUARD

BETWEEN 1967 and 1994 the Palestinian national leadership lived in a diaspora, with the PLO headquarters moving from Jordan to Lebanon to Tunisia. Local leadership in the West Bank and the Gaza Strip, meanwhile, sought to assert itself from time to time, only to be decapitated by the Israelis or discouraged by the PLO. The PLO's defeat at the hands of Israeli soldiers when Israel invaded Lebanon in 1982 lessened its centrality in Palestinian politics and weakened its hold on Palestinians in the occupied territories. Indeed, the center of gravity in Palestinian politics began to shift from the outside to the inside. It was the newly emerging leadership in the occupied territories, for example, that initiated and sustained the first intifada from 1987 to 1993.

In 1994, however, implementing the Declaration of Principles negotiated at Oslo, the PLO leadership returned home to the West Bank and Gaza to establish the Palestinian Authority. Since then, the relationship between the older, established nationalist leadership and the younger, emerging one has not been easy. Efforts by the old guard to co-opt or accommodate the young leaders of the first intifada have not always succeeded, chiefly because of the old guard's authoritarian tendencies. Nonetheless, the euphoria accompanying the partial Israeli withdrawal from occupied Palestinian territory, the holding of the first national elections in 1996, and the establishment of the first Palestinian government in modern history have produced an appearance of harmony.

The old guard is composed of the founders of the Palestinian national movement, together with the leaders of various guerrilla organizations and the PLO bureaucracy. These men, few of whom are under 50, have spent most of their political lives outside the Palestinian territories. This political establishment dominates both Fatah and the PA. Key figures in this group, such as Mahmud Abbas (also known as Abu Mazin), Ahmad Qurie (also known as Abu Ala), and Nabil Sha'ath, have also controlled the Palestinian team in the peace negotiations.

The young guard is composed of newly emerging local leaders as well as the leaders of the first intifada. Most are no older than

40. A few serve in the PA cabinet and the PLC, and as heads or senior members of different security services. But as a whole, the group lacks cohesion, leadership, and formal authority. Indeed, certain younger nationalists are known as gangsters or warlords among some of their fellow Palestinians; others, such as Sami Abu Samhadaneh in Rafah and Aatif Ebiat in Bethlehem, have been targeted for assassination by the Israeli army, and the latter was killed this past October. But certain prominent members of the young guard, such as Marwan Barghouti in Ramallah and Husam Khader in Nablus, are more respectable. Although the young guard has little voice in the main PLO institutions, it has more power in Fatah bodies such as the High Committee and the Revolutionary Council, as well as in Fatah's semi-militia, the Tanzim, and armed wing, al Aqsa Brigades.

The Palestinian political establishment derives its legitimacy from the PLO's historical legacy as well as from the Oslo agreement and its outcome. It controls the financial resources of the PLO and the PA, receives diplomatic recognition from the international community, and controls the PA bureaucracy and security services. The newer political arrivals, however, have drawn strength during the second intifada from their alliance with the Islamist opposition and from overwhelming public dissatisfaction with the progress of peace negotiations and national reconstruction. The insurgents have used these tools to neutralize the old guard's control of official state power. And although the armed wing of the young guard may still be small, it has been able to quietly take control of many of the crumbling PA civil institutions and deter any attempts by the PA security services at a crackdown. The young guard has sought not to create new national institutions but rather to work for control of the existing ones.

The old guard has a clear leadership hierarchy. Arafat does not simply dominate this group; its survival depends on his continued presence and support. The young guard also recognizes Arafat's leadership, but it does not derive its legitimacy from him; indeed, it is Arafat who has felt a need to demonstrate credibility to the younger leaders, by tolerating their alliance with the Islamists and their violent confrontations with the Israeli army. Since March

2001, as Israel has begun targeting the regular PA police and security forces, Arafat has even allowed units from the Presidential Guard and the Palestinian intelligence services to participate in attacks on Israeli soldiers and settlers, despite the risks involved. He apparently feels the alternative method by which to gain the approval of the young guard—opening up the Palestinian political system and encouraging a true transition to democracy—is even less attractive.

But the young guard continues to demand more from Arafat's camp. It wants transparency, accountability, a campaign against corruption, and more direct confrontation with Israel. It has also called for the establishment of a national unity government that would include not only representatives from its own ranks, but also senior members of Islamist and other opposition groups. And it has strongly supported local and international demands for good governance, including respect for the rule of law, an independent judiciary, a stronger role for the legislature, and stronger and more efficient public institutions.

ENDS VS. MEANS

THE YOUNG GUARD strongly opposes any cease-fire agreement that would entail a crackdown on Palestinian nationalist or Islamist militants. Indeed, it has publicly condemned both the Mitchell Report (the conclusions of a fact-finding committee led by former U.S. Senator George Mitchell to look into the recent Israeli-Palestinian violence) and the Tenet Plan (the cease-fire and security plan put forth by Director of Central Intelligence George Tenet in June 2001). Rather than embrace these initiatives for ending the violence, the young guard wants Arafat to "come out of the closet" by publicly endorsing the intifada's goals and methods and by ordering PA security forces to join the armed confrontations. The old guard, on the other hand, doubts the efficacy of violence and is critical of even the minor involvement of some PA security forces in the fighting. Nevertheless, many of its members are convinced that Arafat cannot seriously confront the young guard without a reasonable chance for a peace agreement with Israel, and some accept the argument that on the way to reaching this goal the occasional participation of official security services in the fighting is essential. When the time comes to end the armed confrontations, they reason, only those with a credible record of fighting will have the domestic legitimacy and resolve to confront and detain those who want to continue.

Some members of the old guard outside the PA have sought to distance themselves from the government and establish a new forum for political mobilization and reform. In January 2001, for example, the speaker of the Palestinian National Council, which represents Palestinians in the West Bank and Gaza as well as in the diaspora, demanded that the PA fully address government corruption and the absence of the rule of law, called on the members of Arafat's cabinet to resign, and called for the establishment of a "national independence organization." The young guard did not embrace the idea, however, and has sought to assert itself not through the open condemnation of the PA but rather through defeat of the Israeli army.

As for its ultimate political objectives, despite what some in Israel and the West think, the young guard shares with the old regime the goals of an independent Palestinian state (with Arab East Jerusalem as its capital) living side by side in peace with Israel, and a just solution to the refugee problem. Although most members of the young guard advocate a more hawkish version of this basic position than their older counterparts, their position probably reflects the heightened threat perception generated by daily bloodshed; some members of the group, such as Sari Nusseibeh, the president of al Quds University and Arafat's representative in East Jerusalem, have quite moderate goals with respect to the peace process and oppose pursuing them through violence.

The chief difference between the young guard and the old guard with respect to Israel lies in how they define victory in the battle against occupation. Arafat's group seeks a negotiated settlement that would not only end the occupation but also allow the established leaders to remain in power in Palestine for years to come. By contrast, the young guard does not consider negotiations a necessary part of the equation; a unilateral Israeli withdrawal or separation would suit it just as well. The insurgents could not oppose a negotiated settlement supported by the majority of the Palestinians, should one ever emerge. But they realize that only the old guard can negotiate such a deal, for only it has a unified national leadership and a well-articulated vision, as well as experience and connections with Israelis. So for the young guard, a unilateral Israeli withdrawal or separation is a more attractive way of achieving Palestinian nationalist objectives: in bypassing the negotiations between the Israelis and the PA, it would render the old guard irrelevant and elevate the young guard to power.

At first the PA establishment welcomed the new intifada because it thought the increased pressure on Israel would strengthen its hand at the negotiating table. The young guard, however, saw the uprising as a means to disrupt negotiations rather than pursue them. The failure to achieve a breakthrough at Camp David affirmed these younger leaders' belief that the Palestinians could end the occupation on their own terms only through armed popular confrontation.

To increase pressure on Israel and to strengthen its domestic position, in the first weeks of the intifada the young guard formed an alliance with the Islamists and other opposition forces. Even though they disagree over ultimate objectives, the young guard prefers to have the Islamists in its coalition and under its leadership, not least because it remembers how during the first intifada the Islamists created a parallel leadership, institutional structure, and armed wing.

The generation gap is not the only important division in Palestinian politics and society. The divide between nationalists and Islamists is also crucial, as is a sometimes hidden debate between advocates and opponents of the Oslo peace process. Some young guard members, particularly those already integrated into PA and PLO institutions—along with those such as Nusseibeh who are influenced by the tradition of nonviolence—agree with most of the old guard that the current uprising is a dramatic mistake. Given the current political stalemate and overwhelming popular support for armed confrontation, however, this group has been marginalized and remains quiet.

AT THE CROSSROADS

WHETHER PALESTINIAN domestic tensions are resolved or exacerbated will depend on which of three possible scenarios emerges. If the simmering Palestinian-Israeli impasse continues, the chief beneficiary will be the Islamists. If Israel opts for a significant unilateral withdrawal or separation, however, the young guard will profit. And if the Israeli and Palestinian leaderships can agree on some form of significant negotiated settlement, whether transitional or permanent, the old guard will gain a new lease on life.

The continuation of the status quo would lead to a further drop in Palestinian support for the peace process and the compromises it entails, along with continued high levels of support for the use of violence. The PA's legitimacy would continue to diminish, and the popularity of Arafat would decline along with it. The conflict between the old and young guards would further split and weaken the nationalist camp, with the latter gradually gaining ground on the former as a major leadership shift occurred. Arafat would probably continue in power, but his room for maneuver would be extremely constrained. If he were to disappear from the scene, his exit would hasten the demise of the old guard and lead to infighting among the members of the young guard looking to take their place. Those younger leaders currently integrated into the PA would probably join forces with the young guard and provide foot soldiers, public support, and above all political respectability. Whether Arafat remained or left, however, the general balance of power would continue to shift from nationalists to Islamists, with the latter camp eventually succeeding in becoming the dominant force in Palestinian politics and society.

An Israeli unilateral separation or withdrawal, in contrast, would give an unqualified victory to the young guard. Unilateral separation seems attractive because it does not require a partner on the other side. As they conclude that the Palestinians cannot or will not accept the compromises on offer, many Israelis are becoming convinced that separation is the only way to reduce their country's vulnerabilities. A majority of Israelis today support the idea of building a wall to separate the two communities, although the extent of support for the plan depends on where the line of division would be drawn. The larger the Israeli withdrawal and evacuation, the more lukewarm the support becomes. Nonetheless, the idea has enough backing across the political spectrum to make it a credible possibility.

Any unilateral Israeli withdrawal from Palestinian areas would be compared to the Israeli withdrawal from southern Lebanon in 2000. The old guard would likely behave as the Lebanese government did, whereas the young guard would behave like Hezbollah. That is, the PA would not assume control over the newly evacuated territory and settlements, leaving a newly strengthened alliance of young nationalists and Islamists to declare those areas liberated and use them as bases from which to continue the fight against the Israeli army in the remaining occupied zones.

The young guard would likely scuttle any attempt by the PA leadership to use the occasion of an Israeli withdrawal as an opportunity to restart negotiations. Indeed, the younger leaders would probably try to convert their "victory" into open defiance or displacement of the old guard, thus consolidating their capture of the nationalist movement (although they would retain Arafat until an alternative leadership with more than local credentials emerged). Since the Palestinian public would view a unilateral Israeli withdrawal as a clear victory for the young guard, the fortunes of the nationalists in general would surge and those of the Islamists would fall.

A negotiated outcome, finally, would be the scenario under which the old guard could mount a comeback, because only the established PA leaders could deliver an agreement. And an Israeli-Palestinian accord that found support on the Palestinian street would reassert the PA's leadership. The young guard and the Islamists would try to torpedo the agreement, but in doing so they would be going against popular will. More significant, those young nationalists currently integrated into the PA would join forces with the old guard and support the agreement, rather than defecting to the side of their generational colleagues as they might after a unilateral Israeli withdrawal. If accompanied by domestic political reform, moreover, a negotiated deal with Israel could create conditions under which the older and younger wings of the nationalist movement would unify and undercut the standing of the Islamists.

A WAY FORWARD?

MOST ISRAELIS and Palestinians, not to mention the outside world, would probably prefer the negotiated settlement scenario. But is this outcome even possible at this point? Of the three conceivable kinds of settlement—a comprehensive agreement aimed at ending the conflict, a stabilization package designed to tone down the violence and shore up the status quo, and a transitional agreement that would be somewhere in between—none seems likely today. With strong U.S. and European leadership, however, Arafat and possibly even Sharon might find a stabilization agreement acceptable.

A comprehensive agreement would solve all the issues in dispute, including Jerusalem and refugees, and thereby put an end to the conflict. As the progress made during the post–Camp David negotiations showed, such a settlement is possible. If and when the two sides return to serious discussions, they will probably try to build on and complete the work started with the plan that President Clinton put forth in December 2000 and that was developed at Taba, Egypt, the next month. Merely stating the conditions under which such talks could take place, however, shows how far away they are. For a comprehensive settlement to emerge, three conditions would need to be met, none of which exists today. First, Israelis would need to bring into government a leadership and coalition less wedded to an ideology of greater Israel and willing to withdraw from almost all of the occupied Palestinian territory seized in 1967, evacuate most of the settlements, and accept a land swap to allow the remaining settlements to remain under Israeli control. Second, there would need to be a U.S. administration passionately committed to making the process succeed. And third, the old and young on the Palestinian side must achieve a unity of purpose. (This last condition could be met if the old guard embraced domestic political reform that opened up the political system and created a viable partnership between the two leadership groups.)

Neither the Israeli nor the Palestinian public believes such an agreement is possible, and indeed neither is currently willing to lower its sights and accept the painful compromises that any such deal would require. This fact should lead not to despair but rather to the conclusion that only a strong leadership, with solid legitimacy, could consider taking such a path. If two such leaderships were ever to emerge, their publics would most likely be willing to accept, in the end, the compromises required for an agreement to be concluded—but not a day before they had to.

Palestinians Divided

A stabilization package, meanwhile, could serve only as a stopgap measure aimed at calming the situation, restoring public confidence in the peace process, and facilitating a return to more promising final-status negotiations. Such a package would have to include the following: a cessation of all forms of violence, a return to pre-intifada military deployments, a freeze on settlement building, the implementation of existing interim commitments (most notably PA fulfillment of its obligations and a credible Israeli withdrawal from the territories designated "Area C" under the Oslo agreement, which today represent approximately 60 percent of the West Bank and include sparsely populated areas as well as Israeli settlements and military bases and the roads between them), and an agreement to restart final-status talks. Both Israelis and Palestinians should be willing to support such a deal, as it can be rightly described and sold as a constructive way to carry out measures that both sides have already agreed to.

The current Israeli government might agree to such a package, although getting such approval would probably require far more active involvement by the international community, particularly the United States. A complete freeze on settlement building would not be popular. Also unpopular would be the last of the three redeployments from "Area C" that were mandated by the 1995 follow-up agreement to Oslo, the Israeli-Palestinian Interim Agreement—not least because it would involve the evacuation of a number of small and isolated settlements and outposts in the West Bank. On the Palestinian side, successful implementation of such a deal would require the full integration of the young guard into the political system. Absent such integration, the old guard would have to enforce an unpopular cease-fire against a potentially strong and violent resistance by both its nationalist critics and the armed wings of the Islamist and other opposition groups. Even if the young guard were indeed brought on board, however, some minor violence would likely persist and eventually undermine the attempt at stabilization unless significant progress were taking place simultaneously.

Stabilization would require multinational monitoring as a confidence-building measure. International monitors would make it difficult for the young guard to attack Israeli targets without openly defying and embarrassing Arafat, which they might be loath to do. The deployment of monitors would thus increase the cost of cease-fire violations and increase the odds that the armistice would be self-policed. Monitoring would also help reassure each side about the intentions of the other while providing an independent trigger for the implementation of different phases of the agreement, thus creating incentives for both sides to comply fully.

If four additional components were added to a stabilization package, it could serve as a midterm transition arrangement. These four add-ons would be an Israeli evacuation of the whole Gaza Strip, including the removal of all settlements there; a further Israeli redeployment in the West Bank yielding full contiguity to the Palestinian territories there; the establishment of Palestinian statehood; and an extension of the mandate of international monitors to include the supervision of Israeli force deployments and Palestinian control over international border crossings. Sharon could call this a long-term interim agreement, whereas Arafat might prefer thinking of it as a new and improved mechanism for the implementation of the existing interim agreement, but if the desire were there to move forward, an upgraded stabilization package could be sold to both the Israeli and Palestinian publics.

Shimon Peres, now Israel's foreign minister, has already advocated most of these components, and Sharon has reportedly been willing to discuss the Gaza evacuation since his first visit to the United States as prime minister. He has also repeatedly declared his willingness to accept the establishment of a contiguous Palestinian state. Still, any progress toward a transitional agreement would almost certainly have to come through a more modest stabilization package first.

REFORM OR PERISH

THE SEPTEMBER 11 attacks had a significant but temporary impact on the Palestinian community. International outrage over terrorism and the U.S. determination to lead an alliance into combat against it created new fears while opening new opportunities. Arafat was determined to avoid any association with terror against civilians and eager to show solidarity with the United States. Most Palestinians, including the young guard, feared that

Israel would take advantage of the crisis to launch a devastating attack against the PA-controlled areas. And Palestinian Islamists feared being linked to Osama bin Laden and his network. As a result, the Islamists refrained from suicide attacks against Israeli civilians for a while, the young guard kept its distance from its allies, and the old guard's international credentials became an asset and a useful cover. For Arafat, the cost of continued appeasement of the young guard increased dramatically, and he may well have feared for his own survival.

At the same time, however, the U.S. need for Arab and Islamic support in the war against terror provided opportunities. It was only in the aftermath of the Persian Gulf War, after all, that a U.S. administration could do what was necessary to bring about the Madrid Middle East Peace Conference, which set up unprecedented direct peace negotiations between Israel and all its Arab neighbors. The old guard hopes for something similar this time as well. So Arafat used pressure and persuasion to get his internal opponents to accept a temporary calm.

Neither the young guard nor the Islamists believed Sharon would play along, though, and so far their skepticism has proven justified. Committed to the notion that Arafat's hand is behind every violent incident, Sharon and senior members of the Israeli army and intelligence community seem to have reached the conclusion that Arafat is no longer a partner. Indeed, they may be engaging in a steady but piecemeal process of delegitimation and liquidation of his authority. They understood that the relative calm on the Palestinian side could be only temporary and sought to deny him the potential lifeline that post–September 11 international diplomacy might offer. The Israeli policy of assassination and incursions into territories that it had already handed over has continued, even though Arafat succeeded in reducing the level of violence by more than 80 percent in short order. And it may well be that even well-intentioned outside diplomatic efforts will be unable to force Arafat to make a full commitment to the cease-fire or check Sharon's continued provocations.

Arafat and the old guard are thus unlikely to opt for a full cease-fire and may even lack the capacity to enforce one. Since the eruption of the second intifada they have had to walk a delicate tightrope: the PA no longer enjoys a monopoly over the use of force in its territory, its legitimacy is questioned by the Palestinian street, its public supports violence and opposes cracking down on either the Islamists or the young guard radicals, and no viable political process looms on the horizon. If Arafat acts to suppress his internal opponents he risks being seen, if successful, as an Israeli lackey or even another Sa'd Haddad (the commander of the South Lebanon Army created by Israel in the late 1970s to provide security for northern Israel). And if unsuccessful, he faces a civil war.

His choices are therefore limited. In a changed political environment, one in which Arafat obtains legitimacy and public support, he could move to enforce a cease-fire. Such an environment could be triggered by a jump-starting of the peace process, initiated and led by the United States and supported by the international community, but the odds of this happening are clearly very low.

Yet if the current situation looks bad—especially after the resumption of major Palestinian suicide attacks on Israelis in early December—it is easy to imagine how it could get even worse. Today Arafat's leadership is the glue that keeps the old guard and young guard together, preventing a full and immediate takeover by the latter. Despite his poor communication skills, Arafat continues to give the Palestinian public a sense of stability, thus preventing large-scale breakdown of law and order. His presence deters the Islamists from posing an immediate threat to the shaky dominance of the nationalists; in his absence, all hell could break loose.

Of course, Arafat and the PA have an alternative to this bleak future: instead of waiting in vain for an American or international peace plan to rescue them, they could embark now on a process of political reform. Doing so would allow the nationalist movement to regain the support of most Palestinians while integrating its two central factions. For Arafat, the old guard, and the Palestinian community in general, the message would seem to be clear: reform or perish.✪

The Last of the Patriarchs

Aluf Benn

THE BULLDOZER

JUST OVER a year ago, on March 7, 2001, Ariel Sharon took office as Israel's eleventh prime minister, having beaten his predecessor, Ehud Barak, in a landslide. Sharon's election seemed like the ultimate expression of Israeli anger, the choice of a public frustrated by the stagnation of the peace process and the violence of the second Palestinian intifada. After all, Sharon, known as "the Bulldozer," was the ultimate hard-liner: the builder of the settlements and a warrior who had fought the Arabs for more than 50 years. Indeed, Sharon had been responsible for some of the most controversial acts in Israel's military history, including its 1982 invasion of Lebanon. Now finally at the helm, he vowed not to negotiate under fire and to fight until terror was defeated. Only then, he promised Israelis, would he make what he called "painful concessions" for peace.

Conditions in Israel are now even worse than when Sharon took office. Palestinian terror attacks occur almost daily and have killed more than 250 Israelis in the past year. Israel has responded with a mix of economic sanctions and escalating military actions. These strikes have included recent, massive incursions into cities and refugee camps in the West Bank and Gaza with tanks, troops, and helicopter gunships; Israel even temporarily reoccupied Ramallah with a division-size force. Although more than 640 Palestinians have already been killed in the last year, however, the war of attrition continues with no end in sight. Only a delicate combination of mutual

---

ALUF BENN is Diplomatic Correspondent for *Ha'aretz,* an Israeli daily newspaper. He has covered Israel's foreign policy and the Arab-Israeli peace process since 1993.

deterrence and international pressure has prevented this low-grade confrontation from exploding into an all-out war.

Meanwhile, Israel's economy has fared no better. Growth has ground to a halt, unemployment has shot up, and the shekel has dropped in value. Israel's man of action has seemed virtually paralyzed in the face of economic and political crises.

And yet even with a national disaster looming on two fronts and no apparent solutions, Sharon remained extremely popular during his first year in office. His job approval rating generally stayed between 50 and 70 percent in weekly opinion polls. Only in late February did his ratings begin to drop below 50 percent. The public must be aware of Sharon's flaws—after all, his poor job performance is hard to ignore. Yet, apparently convinced that there are no alternatives, Israelis have stubbornly clung to this 74-year-old national father, one of the few figures remaining from Israel's early days.

Sharon, however, has proven unable to translate his remarkably durable popularity into action. Instead, all his energy has gone into fighting for his political survival. The prime minister faces a seemingly insoluble dilemma. He wants to run again in the November 2003 elections, but to do so, he will first have to reaffirm his leadership of the Likud Party. But this means outflanking his rival, former Prime Minister Binyamin Netanyahu, who has won over many of the party faithful by preaching tougher military measures against the Palestinians. To beat him, Sharon must swing to the right. Yet he remains bound to the left by the need to maintain U.S. support and to hold together his national unity coalition with the Labor Party. Above all, Sharon wants to keep Shimon Peres, a former prime minister and Nobel Peace Prize winner, in office as his foreign minister.

In light of these impossible constraints, it is no surprise that Sharon's first year as prime minister has been characterized by indecisiveness and constant zigzagging between right and left. Urged in one direction by his gut instincts but shackled by politics, even this master tactician seems unable to work out a grand strategy. Instead, Sharon has governed by reaction, not initiative, and has avoided big risks. As a result, he has so far managed to avoid the kinds of major mistakes that marred the tenures of his predecessors, Netanyahu and Barak, and led to their premature downfalls.

In place of vision, Sharon has offered increasing doses of tough language and military blows against the Palestinian Authority (PA) and its leader, Yasir Arafat. And if Sharon has one accomplishment to boast of, it is that he secured strong American backing, which, at least until recently, helped him further isolate his old nemesis, Arafat. Sharon now openly calls for Arafat's replacement—something that would have been unthinkable only a year ago. Yet while keeping Arafat under virtual house arrest in Ramallah, Sharon also became the first Likud leader ever to agree publicly to the creation of a Palestinian state.

So far, the Palestinians have responded to Sharon's pressure by using the heaviest weapons in their arsenal, from suicide bombings in Israeli cities to indigenously produced rockets. Israel has retaliated with air power, temporary invasions of Palestinian towns, and targeted assassinations of dozens of suspected terrorists. Neither side has managed to win the war or bring it to a peaceful conclusion. Instead, this gradual escalation has only brought the country ever closer to catastrophe.

MAN WITH A PLAN?

THE MOST COMMON QUESTION asked about Sharon today is a simple one: Does he know what he's doing? As events spiral from bad to worse, anxious observers at home and abroad wonder if the prime minister actually has a plan for solving the crisis, or if he is simply trying to buy time and survive.

It is no small irony that this question is being asked about Ariel Sharon, of all people. In contrast to most Israeli politicians, who tend to blur their political positions as they climb the ladder to power, Sharon has clung to a narrow ideology for years. And indeed, the short answer to the current question is yes: he does have a plan of sorts, although it does not include the sort of final-status agreement that Palestinians have in mind.

At the core of Sharon's vision lies his map, which he sees as essential to Israel's future security. Under Sharon's plan, Israel would maintain two West Bank "security zones" under its direct control. The wider zone in the east would provide security against invasion (most likely by Iraq) and serve as a buffer between the Palestinian state and Jordan. Sharon once subscribed to the "Jordan is Palestine" school—rooted in the idea that Israel's neighbor, the population of which is already mostly Palestinian, should be the basis of any future Palestinian homeland. In recent years, however, Sharon has changed his mind and now recognizes that an independent (that is, Hashemite) Jordan remains important to regional stability.

Sharon's second envisioned security zone would lie in the western foothills of the Samarian mountains, along the old 1967 border that divided Israel from the West Bank (then ruled by Jordan). This western buffer would "widen the narrow waist" of Israel and allow it to control the underground aquifer beneath it, which supplies drinking water to Israel proper. Current Israeli settlements in the territories would remain in place—after all, they were planted there (many of them by Sharon himself) for security reasons in the first place.

According to Sharon's plan, the Palestinians would get control over everything between the two security zones—albeit with severe restrictions on their sovereignty. Israel would control Palestine's borders with Jordan and Egypt, as well as its airspace and two or three "lateral roads" connecting the two zones. The new state would be demilitarized, banned from joining military pacts, and committed to cooperating with Israel against terrorism. To ensure the contiguity of their state, Sharon would give the Palestinians some additional land and build a system of tunnels and bridges. He would also support rapid economic development in Gaza and the West Bank, which he believes is necessary to reduce Palestinian militancy and national ambitions. Development projects, including a joint Israeli-Palestinian water desalination plant, would be underwritten by international investment. Finally, Sharon's plan calls for "education for peace" in both societies.

Sharon has publicly sketched out these ideas at various times, packaging them as a "long-term interim agreement," an "armistice agreement," or simply a "non-belligerency" pact. As he sees it, only after this plan had been in place a long while (seven years, according to Palestinians who have met with him; Sharon denies having supplied this figure), and only after a "table of expectations" had been fulfilled, would both sides negotiate a final settlement. Thus Sharon has opposed any attempt—including the various new plans now being floated—to move up these ultimate negotiations. As his February 20 speech to the nation and earlier statements suggest, what Sharon really wants is to freeze the status quo—with some symbolic and economic benefits offered to the Palestinians.

DEAF EARS

PERHAPS UNSURPRISINGLY, Sharon has recently discovered that although his plan may sound good to him, no Palestinians are interested in it, even as a basis for negotiations—at least not without a firm Israeli commitment to move quickly into final-status talks. Sharon may feel that the Palestinians would be better off cutting a deal with him than with a potential successor, since he enjoys strong support in Israel and therefore could actually sell a plan to the Knesset and the public. And he has duly presented his ideas to American and other foreign leaders. But so far the Palestinians have not shown much interest, and Arafat has refused to even consider Sharon's offer.

Since both sides have refused to give ground, Sharon has been unable to initiate negotiations. Instead, he has been left to manage the current war on a day-to-day basis, thus giving the impression that he has no clear strategy for ending it.

In the absence of signs that Sharon can break the deadlock, various theories have arisen to explain his apparent inaction. Critics on the left argue that the former general has not changed since his days as the belligerent architect of the Lebanon war. They argue that his real strategy is to destroy the last remnants of the Oslo peace process, do away with Arafat, and dismantle the PA into smaller "cantons" run by local leaders heavily dependent on Israel. And indeed, Israel's recent blows to the symbols of Arafat's rule—such as the Palestinian airport or the PA's broadcasting facilities—have humiliated Arafat and eroded his power, thus giving credence to this theory. So has the fact that Sharon has encouraged his regional military commanders to hold talks with their Palestinian counterparts on a local level.

Many on Israel's right, led by Netanyahu, have dismissed Sharon's inactivity as weakness and have started calling for the reoccupation of the Palestinian territories, the expulsion of Arafat, and increased reprisals against the PA. Sharon, however, has rejected these demands. In mid-February, in fact, he met with Likud parliamentarians and explicitly told them he had no intention of dismantling the PA or reconquering its land. As for Arafat himself, although Sharon has insisted that he is now irrelevant and has toyed with the idea of ousting him in favor of a new, more "pragmatic" Palestinian leadership, he has bowed to the strong opposition of the United States and Europe and hesitated, at least for the time being, to do anything to force his old enemy out.

In fact, both the left and the right in Israel have misinterpreted Sharon's actions. The truth is that he simply has no idea how to end the war with the Palestinians. And indeed, until now, the prolonged low-intensity conflict has helped Sharon hold on to his two most important assets: the national unity coalition and the support of Washington. A diplomatic or military breakthrough could threaten both. The problem, however, is that as the violence has worsened, the Israeli public has grown more and more exhausted and angry and U.S. pressure has mounted. Sharon's holding pattern may not be sustainable for much longer.

THE DEATH OF THE LEFT

DESPITE THE CURRENT CHAOS, Sharon has profited from two precious assets that he inherited from the previous government: a national consensus over Arafat's blame for the failure of the peace process, and a strong popular belief that the Palestinians are indeed out to destroy Israel. These two factors have convinced most Israelis that the current confrontation was unavoidable, the sequel to Israel's war of independence in 1948. This conviction has made the Israeli public much more tolerant of Sharon's stumbling than it might be otherwise.

The effort to blame Arafat for the current conflict began with Bill Clinton and Barak, who convinced most Americans and Israelis that it was Arafat who had rejected the "generous offer" made at the Camp David summit in July 2000—and that he had opted for violence instead. Palestinian negotiators only made matters worse by demanding a right of return for the Palestinians who fled or were expelled from Israel proper in 1948. Israelis, understandably, view such a return as an existential threat, one that would undermine the character of the Jewish state.

The failure of Camp David and of the follow-up negotiations at the Egyptian resort of Taba in January 2001 threw the Israeli left into total disarray, leaving it without an effective leader or agenda. For many years, the left had argued that Arafat and the Palestinian leadership were ready to compromise if only Israel would make the necessary concessions. But when the moment of truth came, Arafat balked and struck his old revolutionary stance. His rejection of an unprecedented offer seemed to undermine the very logic of the Israeli left and the Oslo peace process.

Indeed, many on the left became convinced that there was no point dealing with the Palestinians anymore. The favored alternative became "unilateral separation," a synonym for partial withdrawal from the occupied territories to fortified Israeli borders. A few traditional leftists rejected this idea and continued to cling to the Clinton plan: to establish a Palestinian state in almost all the territories. But this view found little popular support. Meanwhile, Shimon Peres, once a leader of the Labor Party, joined Sharon's cabinet, apparently without any clear policy in mind. In December 2001, Labor chose another former general and the current defense minister, Binyamin Ben Eliezer, as its new head. But Ben Eliezer has yet to build much of a constituency.

The first cracks in the national consensus supporting Sharon have only recently started to appear. The left is finally starting to show signs of revival, with the resurrected peace movement once more calling for full Israeli withdrawal from the territories. This time, however, leftists have focused mainly on human rights abuses by the Israeli army. A few reserve officers have even begun refusing to serve in the territories. Unlike in the past, however, calls for resuming the peace process remain marginal; Arafat's remarkably low credibility with the Israeli public has made the prospect of serious talks practically impossible.

FRIENDS IN HIGH PLACES

SHARON'S staying power can be attributed to another factor as well: timing. His election coincided with a change of administration in the United States, and on taking office, George W. Bush changed the course of American diplomacy in the Middle East from conflict resolution to conflict management. Bush set himself an unambitious goal: mere "regional stability." Having learned the sour lesson of Clinton's peacemaking fiasco, Bush refused to even meet with Arafat, who had been the most frequent foreign visitor to the Clinton White House.

Sharon had also learned to avoid the mistakes of his predecessors. Two previous Likud premiers, Yitzhak Shamir and Netanyahu, fell from power soon after clashing with Washington. Sharon at first seemed headed for just such a clash: he had long been the strongest "America skeptic" in the Israeli leadership, going as far as to oppose the Kosovo war in 1999. But after becoming prime minister, Sharon decided to avoid confrontation with the United States. Somewhat grudgingly, he accepted the Mitchell report—Washington's panacea for the Israeli-Palestinian crisis—even though it called for a freeze in settlement building. He also acceded to the Tenet plan, a security addendum to the Mitchell report. But true to form, Sharon also demanded a "testing period" of seven days without Palestinian violence before entering the Tenet-Mitchell process—thereby making its implementation more difficult. He withdrew this demand in early March only when pressured by a White House impatient to reach a cease-fire; Sharon announced that, given the high level of violence, achieving a week of quiet before talks began no longer seemed possible.

Fortunately for Sharon, cooperating with Washington has not in general proved difficult. Bush's declared reluctance to engage in Middle East peacemaking, in fact, was music to Sharon's ears. Relations were not initially smooth: having recognized Sharon as a potential troublemaker, the White House treated him suspiciously at first, and the State Department tried to micromanage the conflict. But then came September 11. Only days before the attacks on New York and Washington, Bush, bowing to Saudi pressure, had agreed to increase American involvement in the Middle East and launch a new peace initiative. After the attacks, however, Washington lost its patience for states with links to any form of terror. Saudi Arabia and Egypt, which had long pressed the Palestinian cause with the United States, suddenly started looking like nurseries for al Qaeda terrorists—and lost their influence overnight.

Sharon leapt at the opportunity this shift presented, publicly comparing Arafat to Osama bin Laden. When Washington rejected this characterization, Sharon, fearing that the United States would try to buy Arab support for the coming war on terror by pressuring Israel to make concessions, publicly lashed out at what he called Bush's "appeasement" policy. This risky gamble succeeded at first. When Secretary of State Colin Powell outlined America's new policy on November 19, 2001, he called for the creation of a Palestinian state—but refrained from suggesting what its borders should look like or how to resolve delicate issues such as Jerusalem and refugees. The Powell plan also avoided setting the one thing Sharon dreaded the most: a timetable leading up to final-status talks.

The success of the U.S. war in Afghanistan further weakened moderates in the State Department and strengthened the administration's hawks, Sharon's ardent supporters in Washington. As suicide bombings continued in Israel, Bush adopted a new, tougher stance, voicing his support for Israel's "right of self-defense" (that is, its retaliatory operations), while increasing pressure on Arafat to combat terrorists. This pressure redoubled on January 3, when Israeli commandos intercepted the *Karine A,* a ship loaded with weapons from Iran en route to Palestinian territory. Having been shown intelligence evidence of Arafat's involvement, Bush felt deceived by the Palestinian leader, who had sworn that he knew nothing about it. The president came close to a total break with Arafat. Sharon failed to convince Bush to let him do away with his rival outright, but Palestinian credibility sank to its lowest point in Washington, and Sharon's freedom of action was enhanced even further.

This situation began to change again only in early March, when Washington, upset by the increasing violence, once more shifted gears on the Middle East. As the Bush team started preparing for the second phase of its war on terrorism—a probable attack on Iraq—it began to encounter growing opposition in the Arab world. The United States' closest Arab allies, Jordan and Egypt, openly criticized Bush's hands-off approach to the Israeli-Palestinian conflict, and warned Vice President Dick Cheney on his tour through the region that it was Sharon, not Saddam Hussein, who posed the real threat to peace.

Bush decided to send his special envoy, the retired Marine Corps general Anthony Zinni, back to the area—this time with a stronger mandate to mediate a cease-fire. Washington even overcame its traditional distaste for UN involvement long enough to sponsor Security Council Resolution 1397, which called for an immediate end to hostilities and embraced the "vision" of Israel and Palestine living peacefully "side by side within secure and recognized borders." And when Sharon overplayed his hand militarily, warning about the need to "hit hard" at the Palestinians and ordering a bloody invasion of Palestinian towns, both Powell and Bush chastised the prime minister. At the time of this writing, however, it still remains to be seen how far Washington really plans to go—that is, whether the recent American gestures are merely political attempts at damage control or signify an actual reengagement in peacemaking.

B.G. RETURNS

ON THE DOMESTIC FRONT, Sharon's policy over the last year has been based on a commitment to the status quo. After the meteoric rise and fall first of Netanyahu and then of Barak, the Israeli public was tired of self-appointed revolutionaries and warmly endorsed an old, experienced conservative.

One key to understanding Sharon's approach as prime minister lies in his history. Unlike his predecessors, Sharon came of age in the 1940s and 1950s, and in the shadow of David Ben Gurion—Israel's founder and first prime minister. As a young, brash commando leader, Sharon became Ben Gurion's tool of retaliation against Arab terror attacks. Sitting in Ben Gurion's chair today, Sharon still likes to reminisce about the old days, and his eyes glimmer when he talks about special units now operating nightly in Palestinian towns—on missions similar to the ones he used to undertake. In fact, his current policy of hitting PA installations to retaliate for terror attacks on Israelis developed in the 1950s, when the prime minister, "B.G.," would send Sharon to attack police stations in the West Bank. Then, as now, Israel believed that humiliating its Arab enemies would pressure them into curbing terror attacks. In both cases, this strategy has had mixed results: in the

1950s, Israel's retaliations inflamed the regional arms race and eventually led to the Sinai war of 1956, which was followed by a decade of relative quiet. In recent years, meanwhile, retaliations against the PA have had little positive effect.

Retaliation is not the only strategy Sharon has borrowed from his old boss. His domestic policies sound like old Zionist propaganda pledges. He hopes to import a million Jewish immigrants in the next decade, from Argentina and elsewhere, and to use them to settle the Negev Desert. Such goals may be noble, but the Israeli public today cares more about its own prosperity than about the Zionist dream, and it has demanded immediate solutions for pressing economic and social problems—solutions that Sharon has not been able to offer.

A SHIFT IN THE PLOT?

ON JANUARY 30, Sharon invited three top Palestinian officials—Mahmood Abbas (also known as Abu Mazen), the general secretary of the PLO executive committee; Ahmed Qurei (Abu Ala), the speaker of the Palestinian Legislative Council; and Muhammad Rashid, Arafat's financial adviser and close confidant—for dinner at his official residence in Jerusalem. This was the first face-to-face meeting Sharon had held as prime minister with representatives of the other side. Although Sharon himself denied it, Arafat clearly supported the talks, having sent his top deputies into his adversary's den. Not much progress was made, but the meeting had symbolic value for both sides. Sharon was in the process of packing for his fourth American trip in a year and wanted both to show Washington how flexible he could be and to shoot down rival initiatives that had been floated by his coalition partners, Peres and Ben Eliezer. Arafat likewise hoped to recover some of his favor with Washington.

But did the meeting signal something else, a shift in the plot, a sign that even Sharon might blink and back down from his pledge never to negotiate under fire? At the time of this writing, it is too soon to tell, and there has been no obvious change in Sharon's basic approach other than his decision to stop demanding seven days of quiet before entering talks. Instead, he continues to wait either for a more "moderate" Palestinian leader to emerge or for Arafat to agree to talks about

Sharon's own plan. In the meantime, the Israeli leader is determined to outflank rival initiatives, such as the one negotiated between Peres and Abu Ala. This agreement, leaked to the public in late December 2001, would create a Palestinian state immediately after a cease-fire and then lead straight into negotiations on a permanent-status accord. Sharon insists that the timetable envisioned—one year for talks and another year for implementation—is too optimistic, and he warns that it will only defer the conflict to a later date. Arafat doesn't seem to like the proposal much either, and the Americans have likewise responded coldly.

The problem with Sharon's tactic is that, having wasted his first year in office saying no to negotiations, the prime minister no longer has the bargaining power he once did. Sharon returned from his Washington trip in February even weaker than he had been before, having heard his suggestion to replace Arafat rejected by Bush. Desperate to do something in the face of increasing public pressure and escalating violence, Sharon gave an unprecedented address to the nation on February 20. But this, too, fell flat. Dismissed by the media as an empty gesture, his speech did include one new proposal: the creation of "buffer zones with fences" (a new name for the "security zones" he has proposed before) to achieve "security separation" between the Israelis and the Palestinians.

Before taking office, Sharon had opposed separation or unilateral withdrawal as impractical. But now, at the recommendation of his security chiefs, he has agreed to a version of just that (although, to be fair, Sharon's plan falls far short of full unilateral withdrawal; it leaves the settlements intact, for example). Still, Sharon's buffer zones embody an implied threat to the Palestinians: that Israel may decide to draw its permanent borders unilaterally and lock up the Palestinians behind fences.

LEAPFROG

No sooner had Sharon proposed to wall in the territories than a dramatic new development arose, taking everyone by surprise: the Saudi peace initiative. Leapfrogging over the current quagmire, Saudi Crown Prince Abdullah proposed a new deal: full normalization of relations between the Arab world and Israel, in return for full withdrawal to Israel's June 4, 1967, borders (with some minor modifications and with Israel retaining control over the Western Wall in Jerusalem).

Abdullah's initiative, coming at the end of one of the most frustrating periods since the peace process began, has galvanized Middle East diplomacy. The Saudis' real motivation may have had more to do with improving their image with the United States (badly damaged by the fact that 15 of the 19 September 11 hijackers came from the desert kingdom) than with making peace with Israel. Nonetheless, they have laid a bold new vision on the table (albeit one that has been mooted before), creating a fresh context for discussion.

From an Israeli viewpoint, the Saudi initiative, even in its crude form, offers some tempting advantages. First and foremost, it strips the conflict to its bare bones: land for peace. Abdullah has not mentioned the right of return for Palestinian refugees or demanded that Israel give up its nuclear weapons. Instead, he has proposed a simple real-estate deal between the Jewish state and its neighbors. He has also suggested that he might be open to minor compromises and land swaps, to resolve some contentious issues. Moreover, Abdullah's offer brings with it something only the Saudis can provide: oil money and religious legitimacy, conferred by the guardian of Islam's holiest sites.

The main hurdle for Israel, of course, is that under the Saudi deal, it would have to return to its 1967 borders—something every Israeli government since the Six-Day War has pledged not to do. Barak came close, but even he never offered up all of the territory Israel had captured. Sharon will never even consider it; among other things, it would mean evacuating most, if not all, of his beloved settlements.

In many ways, however, Abdullah's formula accepts certain truths that the current intifada has made clear for both sides. Israel will never agree to the return of Palestinian refugees to Israel proper. And the Palestinians will likewise refuse Israel's demand to keep its settlements in the West Bank. Before the outbreak of the current intifada and even during its early stages, both sides seemed somewhat flexible on these issues. But no longer, and Abdullah's plan has the virtue of recognizing that fact.

From Sharon's perspective, however, the prince's initiative is fraught with dangers. The prime minister may attempt to spin it for his domestic audience, arguing that because he stood firm in the face of violence and refused to make concessions under fire, Israel has received a better offer from the Arabs than ever before. But if Sharon rejects the proposal, the Arabs will use it as a reverse Camp David—arguing before the world that this time it was Israel, not Arafat, who rejected a reasonable offer.

Sharon also risks losing ground at home. If the Arab League formally endorses the plan, including its promise of normalized relations, it could serve as a rallying point for the Israeli left—something Labor has lacked ever since the election. This could cause Sharon's coalition to collapse and lead to a groundswell of support for a final-status agreement.

Knowing the risks, Sharon has so far treated the Saudi proposal with characteristic caution. He initially tried to buy time, asking for "clarifications" and hinting at a possible positive reaction. Most likely, however, he will try to treat the Saudi initiative as he treated the Mitchell report, killing it softly, through inattention and foot-dragging.

What we can expect from Jerusalem, then, is more of the same. Sharon will keep trying to win this war of attrition by military means and will try to avoid substantive negotiations unless and until the Palestinians surrender. Knowing that American backing is essential, Sharon will do all he can—including avoiding excessive escalation—to keep Washington on board.

Given that neither Israel nor the Palestinians show signs of imminent collapse, the two adversaries are likely to continue bleeding each other for the near future. As Palestinian attacks escalate, Sharon will face growing pressure to reconquer the territories and rid them of terrorists. Such operations, however, as have recently occurred in Jenin, Balata, and Ramallah are bound to be costly in Israeli, not just Palestinian, blood. And Israel has no clear exit strategy for ending a prolonged reoccupation.

The one factor that might change this scenario is an American operation to remove Saddam Hussein from power in Iraq. Such an initiative could vary Sharon's fate in a few ways. Washington, anxious for Saudi and Egyptian support, may push Sharon into making compromises and starting peace talks—perhaps on the basis of the Saudi proposal. On the other hand, if Arafat repeats his 1991 folly and once again sides with Saddam, Sharon might finally seize the chance to get rid of his enemy.

The Persian Gulf War put an end to the first intifada and led Israelis and Arabs into Oslo. A second round could have a similar outcome. If, however, Israel gets hit by the ricochets—Iraqi missiles in retaliation for American bombing, for example—the attack could work to Sharon's advantage. Even anticipating such an event, Israelis could well decide to reelect their oldest, most experienced leader.

The fact that Sharon has survived this long demonstrates his remarkable capacity for maintaining a broad coalition under pressure. But his domestic challenges remain very serious. The heavy escalation of violence in late February and early March, combined with his slide in the polls, led Sharon to tilt first to the right, as when he called on Israel to "cause many Palestinian casualties," and then to the left, as when he abandoned his demand for seven days of quiet and ended Arafat's virtual house arrest. Such zigzags have caused the first serious rifts in Sharon's coalition; the recent defection of an extreme right-wing party has made the prime minister even more vulnerable to domestic pressure.

Already, Sharon's political adversaries smell his weakness. Ben Eliezer has called for an early election in November, a year before Sharon's term expires. Although Sharon need not agree, Labor could then defect from the government. Sharon might then cobble together a narrow right-wing coalition, but such an alliance would make it extremely difficult to actually govern.

Meanwhile, Netanyahu is increasing the pressure on Sharon from the right. The prime minister is doing all he can to buy himself more time, hoping to hold his coalition intact through this summer's Knesset session and survive in office until 2003. And he may just make it. But as he bides his time, still hoping for a chance to win a decisive victory over his bitter enemy, Sharon's power will wane, and his ability to influence events will continue to diminish—even as his country grows ever more desperate for a speedy recovery.❷

The Last Negotiation

How to End the Middle East Peace Process

Hussein Agha and Robert Malley

CUT TO THE CHASE

SINCE THE COLLAPSE of the Israeli-Palestinian negotiations and the outbreak of the second intifada, two propositions have gained wide acceptance. The first is that trying to find a comprehensive solution to end the conflict has already been attempted—and at this point, if tried again, can only fail. The second is that an interim solution is therefore the only way out of the current crisis and might succeed if properly implemented. The mounting death tolls on both sides seem to confirm the notion that conflict management rather than conflict resolution should be the order of the day, and that now is the time for taking incremental steps in order to rebuild the torn fabric of trust. In fact, now is precisely the time for a U.S.-led international coalition to put forward an end-of-conflict deal.

The idea that only incremental steps can resolve the current crisis flies in the face of the experience of the past decade. Everything Israelis and Palestinians have tried since 1993 has been of the interim sort—whether the Oslo accords themselves, the 1995 Interim accords, the 1997 Hebron agreement, or the 1998 Wye memorandum. However sensible it may have seemed at the start, in practice the incremental approach has demonstrated serious shortcomings.

HUSSEIN AGHA is Senior Associate Member of St. Antony's College, Oxford University. He has been involved in Israeli-Palestinian affairs for more than 30 years. ROBERT MALLEY is Middle East Program Director at the International Crisis Group. Between 1998 and 2001, he was President Clinton's Special Assistant for Arab-Israeli Affairs.

The Last Negotiation

Lacking a clear and distinct vision of where they were heading, both sides treated the interim period not as a time to prepare for an ultimate agreement but as a mere warm-up to the final negotiations; not as a chance to build trust, but as an opportunity to optimize their bargaining positions. As a result, each side was determined to hold on to its assets until the endgame. Palestinians were loath to confiscate weapons or clamp down on radical groups; Israelis were reluctant to return territory or halt settlement construction. Grudging behavior by one side fueled grudging behavior by the other, leading to a vicious cycle of skirted obligations, clear-cut violations, and mutual recriminations.

By multiplying the number of obligations each side agreed to, the successive interim accords increased the potential for missteps and missed deadlines. Each interim commitment became the focal point for the next dispute and a microcosm for the overall conflict, leading to endless renegotiations and diminished respect for the text of the signed agreements themselves. Steps that might have been easy to win support for domestically if packaged as part of a final agreement were condemned as unwarranted concessions when carried out in isolation. Increasingly beleaguered political leaderships on both sides thus were tempted to take compensatory actions: incendiary speeches by Palestinians, building more settlements by Israelis, and from the two parties, a general reluctance to prepare their people for the ultimate compromises. Designed to placate angry constituents, these moves had the unintended consequence of alienating the other side, making a final deal all the more difficult to achieve. Finally, the succession of piecemeal, incremental agreements made it more difficult to mobilize the support of other countries.

Yet another interim agreement could not cure ills that are inherent in the culture of interim agreements. It would not rebuild trust, it would not lead to a durable political agreement, and it would use up considerable local and international energy in the process. The same defects plague plans that call for the immediate establishment of a Palestinian state with negotiations to follow over its size, prerogatives, and other final-status issues. As for the notion of unilateral Israeli withdrawal from parts of the West Bank and Gaza, such a gesture would only add to these problems the real risk of emboldening those Palestinians who believe that Israel can be forced by violence to pull out. As all of these factors suggest, the current confrontation is not an argument in favor of acting small, but rather a call to start thinking big.

ALL THE WAY

HISTORY DEMONSTRATES that the incremental method has failed. Yet because Israelis and Palestinians did not reach an agreement at Camp David in 2000 or at the talks in Taba, Egypt, that followed, because the parties are deemed unripe, because their leaders seem uninterested and the gaps between them seem unbridgeable, proponents of moving toward a final agreement immediately are dismissed as being at best naive and idealistic, at worst desperately out of touch.

In truth, however, the final-status negotiations that took place in 2000–2001 were not an exception to or a departure from the approach that had prevailed since 1993, but rather its extension and culmination—conducted in the same spirit, and with the same vices, as that which prevailed during the rest of the interim period. No common principles guided these latter discussions; instead, a vision was meant to emerge from an incremental process of give-and-take. As a result, neither side was able to rebut its domestic opponents or rally potential supporters behind a comprehensive vision. Negotiators who might have been able to market a comprehensive deal were uneasy defending its constituent parts in isolation. And the parties were unable to rally significant regional or international backing for a clearly articulated package deal.

The process that started at Camp David suffered from another basic flaw: it was predicated on the widespread but erroneous belief that genuine, durable agreements can emerge only from direct negotiations between Israelis and Palestinians. Although this might be true when it comes to interim or technical agreements, it does not hold for a permanent accord. With the stakes so extraordinarily high for both sides, Israelis and Palestinians have been reluctant to put forward or accept proposals that risk undermining their bargaining position absent the certainty of reaching a comprehensive deal.

Indeed, as a result of the character of the parties' interactions, the inherent power imbalance, and the existential nature of their dispute, negotiations between Israelis and Palestinians have now reached the point of diminishing—even negative—returns. Rather than bring the two sides closer, negotiations serve to play up remaining disagreements and to play down the broad scope of actual convergence. The time for negotiations has therefore ended. Instead, the parties must be presented with a full-fledged, non-negotiable final agreement.

The arguments routinely deployed against making an immediate effort to end the conflict are flawed. Some say, for example, that a permanent solution must await the building of trust between the two sides. But the belief that the conflict cannot be ended so long as mistrust persists is a seemingly logical argument that actually stands reason on its head. Mistrust, enmity, and suspicion are the consequences of the conflict, not its cause. A deal should not be made dependent on preexisting mutual trust; the deal itself will create it.

Other skeptics point to the rightward move of the Israeli public in reaction to the intifada and supposed Palestinian intransigence in 2000 and 2001 as an insuperable obstacle to the acceptance of a final-status deal anytime soon. But this same public moved swiftly from supporting the most peace-oriented government in the country's history to electing one of its most aggressive—suggesting that it could swing back just as quickly. Every poll confirms that Israelis want quiet, normalcy, and safety in their everyday lives. If they were presented with a U.S.-backed, realistic, end-of-conflict agreement, in all likelihood most of them would embrace it. The impact that the recently proposed Saudi offer (full normalization in exchange for full Israeli withdrawal from the territories conquered in 1967) has had demonstrates just how hungry Israelis are for a conclusive way out of the quagmire. And just as one ought not read too much into the Israeli public's apparent frustration, so would it be a mistake to read too much into past Palestinian behavior. Neither the substance of the ideas at Camp David and subsequent talks, nor the process by which they were presented adequately tested the Palestinians' readiness to accept a fair, end-of-conflict deal that met their core interests.

Many argue, finally, that as a matter of principle, any political effort must await the end of the violence so as not to reward it. Yet violence is a byproduct of the political relationship between Israelis and Palestinians and cannot be divorced from it. That relationship is unfortunately destined to remain a conflictual one until its core issues have been, or are in the process of being, resolved. It would be a historical anomaly for a conflict between two fundamentally unequal antagonists to be resolved without violence. In that sense, violence is latent in the interim approach as much as it contradicts it. Unless the two parties reached an accord, in other words, Oslo all but ensured that their perceptions and expectations would clash, and from that point on the cycle was bound to become ever more vicious. Israel believes it cannot negotiate under fire, and the Palestinians fear that, absent fire, the Israelis will have no incentive to negotiate. The violence so inconsistent with the spirit of Oslo thus became its natural successor. The only certain way to stop the killing is to offer the parties a tangible and fair way to end the underlying conflict.

LET'S MAKE A DEAL

THE CASE for seeking a comprehensive deal ultimately depends on whether one believes it is possible to design a package that both sides can accept. Such a deal must protect both sides' core interests without breaching either party's "redlines," or non-negotiable demands.

Israel's basic interests are to preserve its Jewish character and majority; safeguard its security and the safety of its citizens; acquire international legitimacy, recognition, and normalcy; maintain its attachment and links to Jewish holy sites and national symbols; and establish with certainty that the conflict with the Palestinians and the Arab states has ended once and for all and that there will be no further claims. These principles translate into a core set of policy redlines: no mass influx of refugees that would upset Israel's demographic balance; Jerusalem as the capital of Israel; recognition of the sacred Jewish link to the Temple Mount; no return to the 1967 borders; the incorporation into Israel of the vast majority of settlers in their current locations; no second army between the Jordan

River and the Mediterranean Sea; and the perpetuation of the Jordan Valley as Israel's de facto eastern security border.

As for the Palestinians, their basic interests can be defined as living in freedom, dignity, equality, and security; ending the occupation and achieving national self-determination; resolving the refugee issue fairly; governing and controlling the Muslim and Christian holy sites in Jerusalem; and ensuring that whatever deal is finally struck is accepted as legitimate by members of the Arab and Muslim worlds. These principles similarly translate into a set of policy redlines: Palestinian statehood, with genuine sovereignty over the equivalent of 100 percent of the land lost in 1967; a solution to the Palestinian refugee problem in which refugees are given the choice of returning to the areas where they or their ancestors lived before 1948; Jerusalem as the capital of their state; and security guarantees for what would be a nonmilitarized state.

A close examination of past Israeli-Palestinian negotiations and informal discussions shows that a solution does in fact exist that would be consistent with both sides' needs. The key concept on the territorial issue is swaps: Israel would annex a minimal amount of land in the West Bank and in return provide Palestine with the equivalent amount of land from Israel proper. These swaps would be based on demographic and security criteria and be designed to preserve the viability and contiguity of both states. Israel would incorporate a large number of its West Bank settlers and the Palestinians would achieve their goal of 100 percent territorial restitution. Physically linking Gaza and the West Bank could be achieved without splitting Israel by providing the Palestinians unhindered access to and control of a safe-passage route connecting the two areas.

On security issues, the essentials are the nonmilitarization of the Palestinian state and the introduction of an international force—led by the United States and initially including an Israeli presence—stationed on Palestinian territory in the Jordan Valley and along the border with Israel. This force would serve as a political deterrent to any attack, thereby enhancing both sides' sense of security. The fact that it would be an international force would meet Palestinian concerns, while the fact that it would, at first, include an Israeli component would help assuage Israeli fears.

Solving the problem of Jerusalem—claimed by both sides as their political and religious capital—will require a deal based on the dual notions of demographic and religious self-governance. In other words, what is Jewish—namely, West Jerusalem and the Jewish neighborhoods of East Jerusalem, including those established since 1967—should become the capital of Israel, and what is Arab should become the capital of Palestine. Each religion would have control over its own holy sites. Provisions would be made to ensure the territorial contiguity of both capitals as well as unimpeded access to each community's religious sites.

The remaining question is the status of the Haram al-Sharif or Temple Mount, which both sides claim as sacred. Israel's priority is to preserve its connection to this holiest of sites, the cradle of Jewish identity. For the Palestinians, the key is to make it plain to their people and the larger Arab and Muslim worlds that the Haram is theirs. One of the fundamental flaws of prior negotiations was that they viewed this issue through the lens of sovereignty rather than focusing on the practical arrangements required to meet both sides' needs. What should ultimately matter is ensuring that both sides have power over that which affects and concerns them most. Control over the Haram would remain in Palestinian hands—where, indeed, it has rested since Israel captured East Jerusalem in 1967. At the same time, Israel—which is less interested in governing the area than in preserving its physical integrity—would be provided with guarantees against any digging or excavation without its express consent. Those guarantees would be backed by the international community and monitored by an international presence.

HOMEWARD BOUND

THIS LEAVES what is perhaps the most vexing topic of all: the question of the Palestinian refugees. With one side clamoring for their right of return and the other adamantly rejecting it, this problem seems like one on which no compromises are possible. Throughout the 2000–2001 negotiations, the Palestinians underestimated the degree to which Israelis associate even a theoretical Palestinian right of return with the prospect of the end of Israel as a Jewish state. Israelis simply cannot comprehend why Palestinian refugees, if given a chance to live in their own country, would instead choose to move to what has become an alien land. The only plausible explanation, in their eyes, is that the Palestinians continue to harbor the desire to undermine Israel's long-term viability as a Jewish state. Given the already uneasy demographic realities in Israel—which now has a 20 percent Arab minority growing faster than the Jewish population—it is no wonder that the idea of an Arab influx rings alarm bells.

If the Palestinians seem blind to Israelis' fears, the Israelis, for their part, have belittled the seriousness of the Palestinians' demand. With two-thirds of the Palestinian people still living as refugees, Palestinian nationalism remains, at its roots, a diaspora movement— born and bred in refugee camps and animated by the desire to recover lost homes and belongings. The sense of injustice at being evicted from their land pervades Palestinians' national consciousness and has defined their struggle—even more than the desire to establish an independent state.

A solution that satisfied the political demands only of the nonrefugees in the West Bank and Gaza while appearing to ignore the moral, historical, and political demands of the refugees, would be inherently unstable. It would have questionable legitimacy, would undermine the new Palestinian state, and—most alarming from an Israeli perspective—would leave open the prospect that a sizeable number of Palestinians would decide to carry on the struggle. Although denying outright the Palestinians' right of return might seem a way to end Israelis' immediate anxiety, it would not end the conflict; it would only transfer the seat of unrest to the Palestinian diaspora without eliminating the threat to Israel's security.

The challenge is to find a stable and durable solution that accommodates both the refugees' yearning to return to the areas they left in 1948 and Israel's demographic fears. This can be accomplished by relying on two basic principles. First, refugees should be given the choice to return to the general area where they lived before 1948 (along with the choice to live in Palestine, resettle in some third country, or be absorbed by their current country of refuge if the host country agrees). Second, any such return should be consistent with the exercise of Israel's sovereign powers over entry and resettlement locations. Many of the refugees presumably want to go back to their original homes. But these homes, and indeed, in many cases, the entire villages where they were located, either no longer exist or are now inhabited by Jews. The next best option from the refugees' own perspective would be to live among people who share their habits, language, religion, and culture—that is, among the current Arab citizens of Israel. Israel would settle the refugees in its Arab-populated territory along the 1967 boundaries. Those areas would then be included in the land swap with Palestine and thereby end up as part of the new Palestinian state.

Together with generous financial compensation and other incentives to encourage refugees to resettle in third countries or in Palestine, this solution would promote several key interests. On one side, Palestinian refugees would carry out the right of return. For them, returning to the general area from which they fled or were forced to flee in the 1948 war would be extremely significant because it would cross an important psychological and political threshold. Although they would not return to their original homes, the refugees would get to live in a more familiar and hospitable environment—and one that would ultimately be ruled not by Israelis, but by their own people. Through the swap, Palestine would acquire land of far better quality than the desert areas adjacent to Gaza that have been offered in the past. For Israelis, meanwhile, this solution would actually improve the demographic balance, since the number of Arab Israelis would diminish as a result of the land transfer. Most important, it would pave the way for a stable outcome in which Palestinians in Gaza, the West Bank, and the diaspora would all have an important stake.

Of course, such a solution would not be problem-free. Israelis might fear that it will add to the anxiety and discontent of the Israeli Arabs who remained under Israeli sovereignty. But the demographic and political problems posed today by the Israeli Arab community already demand urgent attention. How better to neutralize their potentially irredentist feelings than to resolve the broader Israeli-Palestinian conflict?

Some Palestinians might argue that the above plan represents nothing more than a sleight of hand, disguising resettlement in Palestine as a return to their pre-1948 lands. But do the refugees actually want to live in Jewish areas that have become part of an alien country? Would they rather live under Israeli rule than Palestinian rule? And short of calling into question Israel's Jewish identity, is there any other way of implementing the Palestinian right of return?

USE THE FORCE

LURKING behind every dispute over the substance of an Israeli-Palestinian deal is the problem of its implementation. Over the past decade, Israelis and Palestinians have routinely balked at carrying out obligations they have agreed to. Just as routinely, the international community has watched these violations helplessly and done nothing to stop them. Achieving a lasting final-status agreement now will require some means to persuade both parties that this time, commitments will actually be upheld.

A U.S.-led international force would help provide such assurances. This force would do more than merely verify compliance on the ground—although it would do that too, adding an element that has been missing from previous accords. The international force would also act as a neutral broker and referee. It would be the recipient for each side's assets during the initial period of implementation— receiving weapons from the Palestinians, for example, and land from Israel. Handing over valuable assets to a dependable foreign trustee would be much easier for each side than turning them over to a partner deemed untrustworthy. Implementation of these steps could be tied to a transparent system of international incentives and disincentives (such as economic aid to the Palestinians or security assistance to Israel), thus further promoting accurate and timely compliance.

HOW TO GET THERE

The paradox is that, although the outlines of a solution have basically been understood for some time now, the way to get there has eluded all sides from the start. The lesson of the interim period, and the type of final-status negotiations that concluded it, is that relying on the intentions of Israeli or Palestinian leaders is a strategy with scant chance of success. The nature of the conflict, the imbalance of power, domestic politics on both sides, the character of the negotiators, the psychological makeup of the leadership—all these factors have prevented the parties from moving toward a solution.

What is needed to overcome this deadlock is a novel process, a means of waging diplomacy that is independent of the will and whims of the parties' leaderships, one that does not cater to their immediate preferences and that bypasses their immediate constraints. Achieving such a deal will require the forceful intervention of outside actors who can present a package that resonates with both the Israeli and the Palestinian peoples, addressing their fears and concerns and showing that some way out of the impasse is actually possible.

Led by the United States, the effort should involve a broad coalition of European, Arab, and other countries and institutions capable of providing security, as well as economic and political support, to Israelis and Palestinians. The proposal should be sanctioned by a UN Security Council resolution and complemented by a number of third-party arrangements such as a U.S.-Israeli defense treaty, possible Israeli membership in NATO, a pledge by Arab nations to recognize Israel and move toward the normalization of their relations (a process that, to be completed, would also require a peace deal with Syria), American and European security guarantees to the Palestinian state, and a sizable aid package to help build the new state's economy.

The forceful presentation by a U.S.-led international coalition of a deal like the one outlined above would oblige the leaderships of both sides to either sign on or defy the world—along with large segments of their own publics. Indeed, even an immediate negative reply from one or both sides would neither erase the initiative nor rob it of its importance, for the very proposal would marginalize those reluctant to espouse it and set in motion a new political dynamic that, in due course, would force a change of heart among the leaders—or else a change of leaders.

Some will argue that anything coming from the outside will be viewed as a foreign imposition and therefore be rejected. However, if the deal is based on past and present Israeli-Palestinian discussions it will not be viewed as imposed from outside; and if it is fair, it is unlikely to be rejected. This would not be a case of outsiders seeking to force a secretly concocted agreement on unwilling parties, since the core of the agreement will have derived from the parties' own previous interactions. Moreover, the mechanism of ratification should be predicated on popular referenda in Israel and among the Palestinian people and should be built into the proposal itself.

The danger is to believe that what looks practical and down-to-earth—step-by-step rebuilding of the process, resumption of security cooperation, gradual improvements on the ground—is the preferable approach. The incrementalism of the previous decade has proved bankrupt time and again because it was based on a misunderstanding of the nature and dynamics of the conflict. The approach did not fail as a result of the parties' ill will or a lack of faithful implementation; rather, it was the approach that contributed to both.

Seldom has more ink been spilled than over the issue of whether Israeli or Palestinian leaders genuinely want or can make a final deal. These are assumed to be the key questions, the answers to which can unlock the door to a peaceful settlement. But they are not and cannot. The point now should not be to accommodate the Israeli and Palestinian leaders' limitations and shape the effort to fit their proclivities; it should instead be to make the limitations of both sets of leaders irrelevant. As violence continues to threaten and the outlines of a fair agreement lie idly by for all to see, the notion of simply waiting for these leaders to finally negotiate a deal or for the two sides to gradually regain their trust in each other is ringing increasingly hollow. The time has come for an effort that is neither top-down nor bottom-up, but outside-in: the forceful presentation by external actors of a comprehensive, fair, and lasting deal.✿

The Palestinian H-Bomb

Terror's Winning Strategy

Gal Luft

NEVER IN ISRAEL'S HISTORY, to paraphrase Churchill, has so much harm been inflicted on so many by so few. Since the onset of the second intifada in late September 2000, dozens of exploding humans—Palestinian H-bombs—have rocked the Jewish state and transformed the lives of its people. As little as a year ago, suicide bombings were seen as a gruesome aberration in the Israeli-Palestinian conflict, an expression of religious fanaticism that most Palestinians rejected. But in recent months a new, unsettling reality has emerged: the acceptance and legitimation of the practice among all Palestinian political and military factions.

Increasingly, Palestinians are coming to see suicide attacks as a strategic weapon, a poor man's "smart bomb" that can miraculously balance Israel's technological prowess and conventional military dominance. Palestinians appear to have decided that, used systematically in the context of a political struggle, suicide bombings give them something no other weapon could: the ability to cause Israel devastating and unprecedented pain. The dream of achieving such strategic parity is more powerful than any pressure to cease and desist. It is therefore unlikely that the strategy will be abandoned, even as its continued use pushes the Middle East ever closer to the abyss.

GAL LUFT is a former Lieutenant Colonel in the Israel Defense Forces and the author of *The Palestinian Security Forces: Between Police and Army*.

The Palestinian H-Bomb

THE PALESTINIAN endorsement of suicide bombings as a legitimate tool of war was not hasty. At the start of the second intifada, the Palestinians' preferred method of fighting was based on the strategy that Hezbollah used to drive the Israel Defense Forces (IDF) out of southern Lebanon after 15 years of occupation—a mix of guerrilla tactics such as ambushes, drive-by shootings, and attacks on IDF outposts. It was thought that the "Lebanonization" of the West Bank and the Gaza Strip would cause the Israeli public to view these territories as security liabilities (as they had with southern Lebanon), and to pressure the government to withdraw once more.

Palestinian leader Yasir Arafat's division of labor was clear. His political wing, Fatah, authorized its paramilitary units, spearheaded by the Tanzim militias along with segments of the security services of the Palestinian Authority (PA), to carry out a guerrilla campaign against Israeli settlements and military targets in the West Bank and Gaza. The militant groups Hamas and Islamic Jihad, meanwhile, were given the liberty to carry out attacks against civilian targets inside Israel.

From the Palestinian perspective, however, the results of the guerrilla campaign in the first year were poor, especially considering the duration of the fighting and the volume of fire. Palestinian forces launched more than 1,500 shooting attacks on Israeli vehicles in the territories but killed 75 people. They attacked IDF outposts more than 6,000 times but killed only 20 soldiers. They fired more than 300 antitank grenades at Israeli targets but failed to kill anyone. To demoralize the settlers, the Palestinians launched more than 500 mortar and rocket attacks at Jewish communities in the territories and, at times, inside Israel, but the artillery proved to be primitive and inaccurate, and only one Israeli was killed.

Israel's response to the guerrilla campaign, moreover, was decisive. Using good intelligence, the Israeli security services targeted individual Palestinian militants and destroyed most of the PA's military infrastructure. Israeli soldiers also moved back into "Area A," the territory that had been turned over as a result of the Oslo peace negotiations to exclusive Palestinian control, to raze suspected mortar activity sites. At first these incursions met with international rebuke, even from the United States. Secretary of State Colin Powell, for example, denounced the first foray into Gaza in April 2001 as "excessive and disproportionate." But over time the temporary incursions became such a common practice that the international community stopped paying attention. Stung by the lack of progress in the struggle, at the end of 2001 Arafat tried a final gambit, attempting to smuggle in a cache of Iranian weapons on board the *Karine-A*. But Israeli naval commandos seized the ship and turned his ploy into a shameful diplomatic disaster. Thus ended Palestinian emulation of the "Hezbollah model."

Unlike the guerrilla strategy, meanwhile, the terror campaign carried out by Hamas and Islamic Jihad was showing results. The Islamic movements managed to kill or maim more Israelis in 350 stabbings, shootings, and bombings inside Israel than the mainstream Palestinian organizations had in more than 8,000 armed attacks in the West Bank and Gaza. The strongest impact came from 39 suicide attacks that killed 70 Israelis and wounded more than 1,000 others. If one compares this bloodshed with the limited damage caused by the 39 Scud missiles Saddam Hussein launched at Israel in 1991— 74 fatalities, most of them caused by heart attacks—it is not hard to understand why the new methods caused such intoxication.

Palestinians are fully aware of what they have suffered at the hands of the Israeli military in response to the terror campaign, but most view it as a great success nevertheless. They derive comfort and satisfaction from the fact that the Jews are also suffering. The Palestinians view the campaign's greatest achievement as not just the killing of so many Israelis but the decline of Israel's economy, the destruction of its tourism industry, and the demoralization of its people. According to a mid-May poll, two-thirds of Palestinians say that the second intifada's violence has achieved more for them than did the previous years of negotiations.[1]

---

[1] Details of the poll and survey methodology are available at the Web site of the Palestinian Center for Policy and Survey Research (www.pcpsr.org).

The Palestinian H-Bomb

LEGITIMIZING TERROR

BEFORE THE OUTBREAK of the second intifada, Palestinians distinguished among attacks on settlers, on Israeli military targets, and on civilians inside Israel. Now, however, those distinctions are disappearing. Although after the Israeli incursions this spring support for attacks against civilians inside Israel dropped 6 points to 52 percent, opposition to arresting those carrying out such attacks rose 10 points to 86 percent—a figure close to the 89 percent and 92 percent support for attacks on Israeli settlers and soldiers in the territories, respectively.

In the post-9/11 era, however, when deliberate attacks against innocent civilians are anathema to most people, embracing terrorism as a strategy has required the Palestinians to persuade themselves, and others, that what they are doing is legitimate. They have therefore created what they see as a moral equivalence between Israel's harm to the Palestinian civilian population and Palestinian attacks against Israeli civilians, including children.

They have also developed a creative interpretation of what terrorism is, one that stresses ends rather than means. Thus, in December 2001, more than 94 percent of Palestinians told pollsters that they viewed Israeli incursions into Area A as acts of terror, while 82 percent refused to characterize the killing of 21 Israeli youths outside a Tel Aviv disco six months earlier that way. And 94 percent reported that they would characterize a hypothetical Israeli use of chemical or biological weapons against Palestinians as terrorism, whereas only 26 percent would say the same about Palestinian use of those weapons against Israel. Interestingly, the new definition extends beyond the conflict with Israel. Only 41 percent of Palestinians, for example, viewed the September 11 attacks as terrorism, and only 46 percent saw the Lockerbie bombing that way.

The more enchanted Palestinians have become with the achievements of their "martyrs," the more Fatah has found itself under pressure to adopt the suicide weapon. Last year, fearing a loss of popular support if the "street" perceived the Islamists' methods as more effective than Fatah's tack, Fatah leaders decided they had to follow suit. The part of Arafat that wanted to show solidarity with the United States and that was determined to avoid any association with terror against civilians, in other words, succumbed to the anti-Israel rage and political calculations of his lieutenants and the members of what Palestinian pollster Khalil Shikaki has called the "young guard" of Palestinian nationalism.

Fatah's official espousal of "martyrdom" operations took place on November 29, 2001, when two terrorists blew themselves up together on a bus near the Israeli city of Hadera. One, Mustafa Abu Srieh, was from Islamic Jihad; the other, Abdel Karim Abu Nafa, served with the Palestinian police in Jericho. But the bond of blood with the Islamists did not last long, and soon Fatah's al Aqsa Martyrs Brigades and the Islamists found themselves engaged in a diabolical contest over which group could perfect the use of the suicide weapon and be viewed as most valuable to the war effort. Al Aqsa has capitalized on the Islamists' opposition to the participation of women and established squads of willing female suicide bombers named after Wafa Idris, the Palestinian woman who blew up herself and an Israeli man in Jerusalem in January. Islamic Jihad, for its part, has recruited children as young as 13 for suicide missions.

Both Islamists and secular Palestinians have come to see suicide bombing as a weapon against which Israel has no comprehensive defense. To counter the Iraqi Scuds, Israel developed and deployed the Arrow, a $2 billion ballistic missile defense system. Against Palestinian H-bombs, Israel can at best build a fence. The suicide bombers are smarter than Scuds, and Palestinians know that even though in Israel today there are more security guards than teachers or doctors, the bomber will always get through.

MILITARY BLINDERS

IF HISTORY is any guide, Israel's military campaign to eradicate the phenomenon of suicide bombing is unlikely to succeed. Other nations that have faced opponents willing to die have learned the hard way that, short of complete annihilation of the enemy, no military solution will solve the problem.

The Palestinian H-Bomb

But the Israeli authorities are deeply reluctant to accept this reality. Israeli society seeks absolute security and adheres to the notion that military power can resolve almost any security problem. If the Palestinians put their faith in Allah, Israelis put theirs in a tank. Whether consciously or not, their belief in the utility of force—evident in the popular "Let the IDF Win" campaign, which advocated a freer hand for the army—reflects a strategic choice to militarize the conflict rather than politicize it. The IDF's senior leaders repeatedly claim that the smart application of military force can create a new reality on the ground that, in turn, will allow the government to negotiate political agreements under more favorable terms.

It is true that when the IDF was finally allowed to "win," Israel achieved impressive tactical results. Operation Defensive Shield this past April eliminated an entire echelon of terrorist leaders in the West Bank, crippled the PA's financial and operational infrastructure, and reduced PA arsenals. But as at other times in its history, Israel failed to convert its tactical achievements into strategic gains. Its intensive use of military instruments earned it international condemnation, further radicalized Palestinian society, and created an environment of anger conducive to more terrorist activities. By May, unsurprisingly, the suicide bombings had started again.

IDF simulations before the second intifada had predicted that a military reentry into major Palestinian cities would lead to hundreds of Israeli casualties. In fact, however, the incursions into territories under Palestinian control proved to be almost painless. Following the assassination of Israel's tourism minister, Rehavam Ze'evi, in October 2001, the IDF launched a broad assault on the PA, entering all six major West Bank cities. Palestinian resistance was negligible, and only six Israeli soldiers were wounded. Operation Defensive Shield, the second big incursion into Area A, also met relatively weak resistance. Aside from the struggle in the Jenin refugee camp, in which 23 Israeli soldiers were killed, Israeli forces conquered six Palestinian cities and dozens of smaller towns and villages while suffering only three fatalities.

The IDF has interpreted the Palestinian lack of resistance in the cities as a sign of weakness rather than a strategic choice. Israelis view with disdain the Palestinian "victory" celebrations after each incursion comes to an end. They are puzzled by the fact that their enemy fires more bullets into the air than at Israeli troops. What Israel fails to comprehend is the paradigm by which the Palestinians are choosing to conduct their war.

Acknowledging their perpetual conventional inferiority, Arafat's people feel no need to demonstrate strong resistance to Israeli forces. They simply wait for the storm to pass while preparing another batch of "martyrs." Families of suicide bombers now receive more than double the financial compensation than do the families of those killed by other means. Nurturing an ethos of heroism fundamentally opposed to that of the Israelis, the Palestinian war of liberation has elevated the suicide bomber to the highest throne of courage and devotion to the national cause.

FENCING LESSONS

ISRAELIS' MISUNDERSTANDING of the new Palestinian way of war may come back to haunt them. Their perception of their enemy's weakness is likely to embolden them and encourage more broad punitive operations in response to future attacks. But Israel's military responses will eventually exhaust themselves, whereas the Palestinians will still have legions of willing "martyrs."

In fact, despite defiant Israeli rhetoric insisting that there will be no surrender to terrorism, one can already see the opposite happening. Israelis are willing to pay an increasingly high economic and diplomatic price for increasingly short periods of calm. As a result, more and more people support panaceas such as unilateral separation—the building of walls, fences, and buffer zones to protect Israel's population centers from Palestinian wrath.

Unilateral separation would no doubt make the infiltration of suicide bombers into Israel more difficult, but it would also increase their prestige in the eyes of many in the region. The bombers would be viewed, correctly, as the catalyst that drove the Israelis out of an occupied territory yet again, and the years of agony Palestinians have endured would be sweetened by a genuine sense of victory. Israel's wall policy, perceived as withdrawal, would reassure the Palestinians that war succeeded where diplomacy failed.

As currently conceived, moreover, walling off the territories would not do much to reduce Palestinian grievances. No matter how long the fence, for example, dozens of Jewish settlements scattered on the hills of the West Bank would necessarily remain beyond it. Two-thirds of Israelis, according to recent polls, support the removal of such isolated and indefensible settlements to make the separation more feasible. But despite such views, Israeli Prime Minister Ariel Sharon has reiterated his refusal to dismantle a single settlement. "The fate of Netzarim is the fate of Tel Aviv," he said recently, referring to the tiny, isolated, and fortified Gaza Strip settlement that has been the target of repeated Palestinian attacks.

DEFUSING THE BOMB

ISRAEL finds itself, therefore, at a crucial turning point in its history, but one from which no path seems particularly attractive. It must find some way of defending itself against an enemy so eager to inflict pain that it is willing to bring suffering and death on itself in the process. Retaliation is unlikely to work, but retreat is likely only to bring more of the same.

If there is any way out of this dilemma, it may lie in convincing the Palestinian public that its constructive goals can be achieved only by relinquishing its destructive strategy. Israel should therefore embark on a policy that rewards the Palestinians for genuinely fighting terrorism and avoid any policy that feeds the perception that terrorism works.

The rewards will have to be tangible and meaningful. Israel could, for example, offer the PA the removal of a number of small hilltop settlements in exchange for a period of non-belligerency and unequivocal renunciation of suicide bombing. This cooling-off period could then set the stage for renewed talks on a final-status agreement. Such an approach would indicate to the Palestinian population that Israel is serious about peace and ready to pay the necessary price for it, not only in words but in deeds. Most important, showing that Israel is prepared to confront and rein in its own radical rejectionists would put the onus on the Palestinian leadership to do the same.

Before this intifada, a large majority of Palestinians opposed attacks against civilians inside Israel. They hoped to achieve their aspirations for independence without resort to terror. Figuring out how to make that happen is not only the right thing to do, but it is also the best way to ensure Israel's security. Unless that hope can be revived, the fate of Tel Aviv could indeed become that of Netzarim—which would be a tragedy for all.◉

The United States and
the Middle East

The Sentry's Solitude

Fouad Ajami

PAX AMERICANA IN THE ARAB WORLD

FROM ONE END of the Arab world to the other, the drumbeats of anti-Americanism had been steady. But the drummers could hardly have known what was to come. The magnitude of the horror that befell the United States on Tuesday, September 11, 2001, appeared for a moment to embarrass and silence the drummers. The American imperium in the Arab-Muslim world hatched a monster. In a cruel irony, a new administration known for its relative lack of interest in that region was to be pulled into a world that has both beckoned America and bloodied it.

History never repeats itself, but when Secretary of State Colin Powell came forth to assure the nation that an international coalition against terrorism was in the offing, Americans recalled when Powell had risen to fame. "First, we're going to cut it off, then we're going to kill it," he had said of the Iraqi army in 1991. There had been another coalition then, and Pax Americana had set off to the Arab world on a triumphant campaign. But those Islamic domains have since worked their way and their will on the American victory of a decade ago. The political earth has shifted in that world. The decade was about the "blowback" of the war. Primacy begot its nemesis.

America's Arab interlocutors have said that the region's political stability would have held had the United States imposed a settlement of the Israeli-Palestinian conflict—and that the rancid anti-Americanism now evident in the Arab world has been called up by

---

FOUAD AJAMI is Majid Khadduri Professor and Director of Middle East Studies at The School of Advanced International Studies, Johns Hopkins University.

the fury of the second intifada that erupted in September 2000. But these claims misread the political world. Long before the second intifada, when Yasir Arafat was still making his way from political exile to the embrace of Pax Americana, there was a deadly trail of anti-American terror. Its perpetrators paid no heed to the Palestinian question. What they thought of Arafat and the metamorphosis that made him a pillar of President Clinton's Middle East policy is easy to construe.

The terror was steady, and its geography and targets bespoke resourcefulness and audacity. The first attack, the 1993 truck bombing of the World Trade Center, was inspired by the Egyptian cleric Sheikh Omar Abdel Rahman. For the United States, this fiery preacher was a peculiar guest: he had come to *bilad al-Kufr* (the lands of unbelief) to continue his war against the secular regime of Egyptian President Hosni Mubarak. The sheikh had already been implicated in the 1981 murder of Mubarak's predecessor, Anwar al-Sadat. The young assassins had sought religious guidance from him—a writ for tyrannicide. He had provided it but retained a measure of ambiguity, and Egypt let him leave the country. He had no knowledge of English and did not need it; there were disciples and interpreters aplenty around him. An American imperium had incorporated Egypt into its order of things, which gave the sheikh a connection to the distant power.

The preacher could not overturn the entrenched regime in his land. But there was steady traffic between the United States and Egypt, and the armed Islamist insurgency that bedeviled Cairo inspired him. He would be an Ayatollah Khomeini for his followers, destined to return from the West to establish an Islamic state. In the preacher's mind, the world was simple. The dictatorial regime at home would collapse once he snapped its lifeline to America. American culture was of little interest to him. Rather, the United States was a place from which he could hound his country's rulers. Over time, Abdel Rahman's quest was denied. Egypt rode out the Islamist insurgency after a terrible drawn-out fight that pushed the country to the brink. The sheikh ended up in an American prison. But he had lit the fuse. The 1993 attack on the World Trade Center that he launched was a mere dress rehearsal for the calamity of September 11, 2001. Abdel Rahman had shown the way—and the future.

There were new Muslim communities in America and Europe; there was also money and freedom to move about. The geography of political Islam had been redrawn. When Ayatollah Khomeini took on American power, there had been talk of a pan-Islamic brigade. But the Iranian revolutionaries were ultimately concerned with their own nation-state. And they were lambs compared with the holy warriors to come. Today's warriors have been cut loose from the traditional world. Some of the leaders—the Afghan Arabs—had become restless after the Afghan war. They were insurrectionists caught in no man's land, on the run from their homelands but never at home in the West. In Tunisia, Egypt, and Algeria, tenacious Islamist movements were put down. In Saudi Arabia, a milder Islamist challenge was contained. The counterinsurgencies had been effective, so the extremists turned up in the West. There, liberal norms gave them shelter, and these men would rise to fight another day.

The extremists acquired modern means: frequent flyer miles, aviation and computer skills, and ease in Western cities. They hated the United States, Germany, and France but were nonetheless drawn to them. They exalted tradition and faith, but their traditions could no longer give them a world. Islam's explosive demography had spilled into the West. The militant Islamists were on the move. The security services in their home countries were unsentimental, showing no tolerance for heroics. Men like Abdel Rahman and Osama bin Ladin offered this breed of unsettled men a theology of holy terror and the means to live the plotter's life. Bin Ladin was possessed of wealth and high birth, the heir of a merchant dynasty. This gave him an aura: a Ché Guevara of the Islamic world, bucking the mighty and getting away with it. A seam ran between America and the Islamic world. The new men found their niche, their targets, and their sympathizers across that seam. They were sure of America's culpability for the growing misery in their lands. They were sure that the regimes in Saudi Arabia and Egypt would fall if only they could force the United States to cast its allies adrift.

NOT IN MY BACKYARD

TERROR shadowed the American presence in the Middle East throughout the 1990s: two bombings in Saudi Arabia, one in Riyadh in November of 1995, and the other on the Khobar Towers near Dhahran in June of 1996; bombings of the U.S. embassies in Tanzania and Kenya in 1998; the daring attack on the U.S.S. *Cole* in Yemen in October 2000. The U.S. presence in the Persian Gulf was under assault.

In this trail of terror, symbol and opportunity were rolled together—the physical damage alongside a political and cultural message. These attacks were meant for a watchful crowd in a media age. Dhahran had been a creature of the U.S. presence in Saudi Arabia ever since American oil prospectors turned up in the 1930s and built that city in the American image. But the world had changed. It was in Dhahran, in the 1990s, that the crews monitoring the no-fly zone over Iraq were stationed. The attack against Dhahran was an obvious blow against the alliance between the United States and Saudi Arabia. The realm would not disintegrate; Beirut had not come to Arabia. But the assailants—suspected to be an Iranian operation that enlisted the participation of Saudi Shi`a—had delivered the blow and the message. The foreigner's presence in Arabia was contested. A radical Islamist opposition had emerged, putting forth a fierce, redemptive Islam at odds with the state's conservative religion.

The ulama (clergy) had done well under the Saud dynasty. They were the dynasty's partners in upholding an order where obedience to the rulers was given religious sanction. No ambitious modernist utopia had been unleashed on them as it had in Gamal Abdel al-Nasser's Egypt and Iran under the Pahlavis. Still, the state could not appease the new breed of activists who had stepped forth after the Gulf War to hound the rulers over internal governance and their ties to American power. In place of their rulers' conservative edifice, these new salvationists proposed a radical order free from foreign entanglements. These activists were careful to refrain from calling for the outright destruction of the House of Saud. But sedition was in the air in the mid-1990s, and the elements of the new utopia were easy to discern. The Shi`a minority in the eastern province would be decimated and the Saudi liberals molded on the campuses of California and Texas would be swept aside in a zealous, frenzied campaign. Traffic with the infidels would be brought to an end, and those dreaded satellite dishes bringing the West's cultural "pollution" would be taken down. But for this to pass, the roots of the American presence in Arabia would have to be extirpated—and the Americans driven from the country.

The new unrest, avowedly religious, stemmed from the austerity that came to Saudi Arabia after Desert Storm. If the rulers could not subsidize as generously as they had in the past, the foreigner and his schemes and overcharges must be to blame. The dissidents were not cultists but men of their society, half-learned in Western sources and trends, picking foreign sources to illustrate the subjugation that America held in store for Arabia. Pamphleteering had come into the realm, and rebellion proved contagious. A dissident steps out of the shadows, then respectable critics, then others come forth. Xenophobic men were now agitating against the "crusaders" who had come to stay. "This has been a bigger calamity than I had expected, bigger than any threat the Arabian Peninsula had faced since God Almighty created it," wrote the religious scholar Safar al-Hawali, a master practitioner of the paranoid style in politics. The Americans, he warned, had come to dominate Arabia and unleash on it the West's dreaded morals.

Saudi Arabia had been free of the anticolonial complex seen in states such as Algeria, Egypt, Syria, and Iraq. But the simplicity of that Arabian-American encounter now belonged to the past. A *fatwa* (Islamic decree) of the senior religious jurist in the realm, Sheikh Abdelaziz ibn Baz, gave away the hazards of the U.S. presence in Arabia. Ibn Baz declared the Khobar bombing a "transgression against the teachings of Islam." The damage to lives and property befell many people, "Muslims and others alike," he wrote. These "non-Muslims" had been granted a pledge of safety. The sheikh found enough scripture and tradition to see a cruel end for those who pulled off the "criminal act." There was a saying attributed to the Prophet Muhammad: "He who killed an ally will never know the smell of paradise." And there was God's word in the

Koran: "Those that make war against Allah and his apostle and spread disorder in the land shall be put to death or crucified or have their hands and feet cut off on alternate sides; or be banished from the country. They shall be held to shame in this world and sternly punished in the next." The sheikh permitted himself a drapery of decency. There was no need to specify the identity of the victims or acknowledge that the Americans were in the land. There had remained in the jurist some scruples and restraints of the faith.

In ibn Baz's world, faith was about order and a dread of anarchy. But in the shadows, a different version of the faith was being sharpened as a weapon of war. Two years later, bin Ladin issued an incendiary *fatwa* of his own—a call for murder and holy warfare that was interpreted in these pages by the historian Bernard Lewis. Never mind that by the faith's strictures and practice, bin Ladin had no standing to issue religious decrees. He had grabbed the faith and called on Muslims to kill "Americans and their allies ... in any country in which it is possible to do so." A sacred realm apart, Arabia had been overrun by Americans, bin Ladin said. "For more than seven years the United States has been occupying the lands of Islam in the holiest of its territories, Arabia, plundering its riches, overwhelming its rulers, humiliating its people, threatening its neighbors, and using its peninsula as a spearhead to fight the neighboring Islamic peoples." Xenophobia of a murderous kind had been dressed up in religious garb.

INTO THE SHADOWS

THE ATTACK on the *Cole* on October 12, 2000, was a case apart. Two men in a skiff crippled the *Cole* as it docked in Aden to refuel. Witnesses say that the assailants, who perished with their victims, were standing erect at the time of the blast, as if in some kind of salute. The United States controlled the sea lanes of that world, but the nemesis that stalked it on those shores lay beyond America's reach. "The attack on the U.S.S. *Cole* ... demonstrated a seam in the fabric of efforts to protect our forces, namely transit forces," a military commission said. But the official language could not describe or name the furies at play.

The attack on the *Cole* illuminated the U.S. security dilemma in the Persian Gulf. For the U.S. Navy, Yemen had not been a particularly easy or friendly setting. It had taken a ride with Saddam Hussein during the Gulf War. In 1994, a brutal war had been fought in Yemen between north and south, along lines of ideology and tribalism. The troubles of Yemen were bottomless. The government was barely in control of its territory and coastline. Aden was a place of drifters and smugglers. Moreover, the suspected paymaster of anti-American terror, bin Ladin, had ancestral roots in Hadramawt, the southeastern part of Yemen, and he had many sympathizers there.

It would have been prudent to look at Yemen and Aden with a jaundiced eye. But by early 1999, American ships had begun calling there. U.S. officials had no brilliant options south of the Suez Canal, they would later concede. The ports of call in Sudan, Somalia, Djibouti, and Eritrea were places where the "threat conditions" were high, perhaps worse than in Yemen. The United States had a privileged position in Saudi Arabia, but there had been trouble there as well for U.S. forces: the terrorist attacks in 1995 and 1996, which took 24 American lives. American commanders and planners knew the hazards of Yemen, but the U.S. Navy had taken a chance on the country. Terrorists moved through Yemen at will, but American military planners could not find ideal refueling conditions in a region of great volatility. This was the imperial predicament put in stark, cruel terms.

John Burns of *The New York Times* sent a dispatch of unusual clarity from Aden about the *Cole* and the response on the ground to the terrible deed. In Yemen, the reporter saw "a halting, half-expressed sense of astonishment, sometimes of satisfaction and even pleasure, that a mighty power, the United States, should have its Navy humbled by two Arab men in a motorized skiff." Such was imperial presence, the Pax Americana in Arab and Muslim lands.

There were men in the shadows pulling off spectacular deeds. But they fed off a free-floating anti-Americanism that blows at will and knows no bounds, among Islamists and secularists alike. For the crowds in Karachi, Cairo, and Amman, the great power could never get it right. A world lacking the tools and the political space for free inquiry fell back on anti-Americanism. "I talk to my daughter-in-law so my neighbor can hear me," goes an Arabic maxim. In the fury with which the intellectual and political class railed against the United States and Israel, the agitated were speaking to and of their own rulers. Sly and cunning men, the rulers knew and understood the game. There would be no open embrace of America, and no public defense of it. They would stay a step ahead of the crowd and give the public the safety valve it needed. The more pro-American the regime, the more anti-American the political class and the political tumult. The United States could grant generous aid to the Egyptian state, but there would be no dampening of the anti-American fury of the Egyptian political class. Its leading state-backed dailies crackled with the wildest theories of U.S.-Israeli conspiracies against their country.

On September 11, 2001, there was an unmistakable sense of glee and little sorrow among upper-class Egyptians for the distant power—only satisfaction that America had gotten its comeuppance. After nearly three decades of American solicitude of Egypt, after the steady traffic between the two lands, there were no genuine friends for America to be found in a curiously hostile, disgruntled land.

Egyptians have long been dissatisfied with their country's economic and military performance, a pain born of the gap between Egypt's exalted idea of itself and the poverty and foreign dependence that have marked its modern history. The rage against Israel and the United States stems from that history of lament and frustration. So much of Egypt's life lies beyond the scrutiny and the reach of its newspapers and pundits—the ruler's ways, the authoritarian state, the matter of succession to Mubarak, the joint military exercises with U.S. and Egyptian forces, and so on. The animus toward America and Israel gives away the frustration of a polity raging against the hard, disillusioning limits of its political life.

In the same vein, Jordan's enlightened, fragile monarchy was bound to the United States by the strategic ties that a skilled King Hussein had nurtured for decades. But a mood of anger and seething radicalism had settled on Jordan. The country was increasingly poorer, and the fault line between Palestinians and East Bankers was a steady source of mutual suspicion. If the rulers made peace with Israel, "civil society" and the professional syndicates would spurn it. Even though the late king had deep ties with the distant imperial power, the country would remain unreconciled to this pro-American stance. Jordan would be richer, it was loudly proclaimed, if only the sanctions on Iraq had been lifted, if only the place had been left to gravitate into Iraq's economic orbit. Jordan's new king, Abdullah II, could roll out the red carpet for Powell when the general turned up in Jordan recently on a visit that had the distinct sense of a victory lap by a soldier revisiting his early triumph. But the throngs were there with placards, and banners were aloft branding the visitor a "war criminal." This kind of fury a distant power can never overcome. Policy can never speak to wrath. Step into the thicket (as Bill Clinton did in the Israeli-Palestinian conflict) and the foreign power is damned for its reach. Step back, as George W. Bush did in the first months of his presidency, and Pax Americana is charged with abdication and indifference.

THE SIEGE

THE POWER secured during Desert Storm was destined not to last. The United States could not indefinitely quarantine Iraq. It was idle to think that the broad coalition cobbled together during an unusually perilous moment in 1990–91 would stand as a permanent arrangement. The demographic and economic weight of Iraq and Iran meant that those countries were bound to reassert themselves. The United States had done well in the Persian Gulf by Iraq's brazen revisionism and the Iranian Revolution's assault on its neighboring states. It had been able to negotiate the terms of the U.S. presence—the positioning of equipment in the oil states, the establishment of a tripwire in Kuwait, the acceptance of an American troop presence on the Arabian Peninsula—at a time when both Iran and Iraq were on a rampage. Hence the popular concerns that had hindered the American presence in the Persian Gulf were brushed aside in the 1990s. But this lucky run was bound to come to an end. Iraq steadily chipped away at the sanctions, which over time were seen as nothing but an Anglo-American siege of a brutalized Iraqi population.

The campaign against Saddam Hussein had been waged during a unique moment in Arab politics. Some Muslim jurists in Saudi Arabia and Egypt even ruled that Saddam had run afoul of Islam's strictures, and that an alliance with foreign powers to check his aggression and tyranny was permissible under Islamic law. A part of the Arabian Peninsula that had hitherto wanted America "over the horizon" was eager to have American protection against a "brother" who had shredded all the pieties of pan-Arab solidarity. But the Iraqi dictator hunkered down, outlasting the foreign power's terrible campaign. He was from the neighborhood and knew its rules. He worked his way into the local order of things.

The Iraqi ruler knew well the distress that settled on the region after Pax Americana's swift war. All around Iraq, the region was poorer: oil prices had slumped, and the war had been expensive for the oil states that financed it. Oil states suspected they were being overbilled for military services and for weapons that they could not afford. The war's murky outcome fed the belief that the thing had been rigged all along, that Saddam Hussein had been lured into Kuwait by an American green light—and then kept in power and let off the hook—so that Pax Americana would have the pretext for stationing its forces in the region. The Iraqi ruler then set out to show the hollowness of the hegemony of a disinterested American imperium.

A crisis in 1996 laid bare the realities for the new imperium. Saddam Hussein brazenly sent his squads of assassins into the "safe haven" that the United States had marked out for the Kurds in northern Iraq after Desert Storm. He sacked that region and executed hundreds who had cast their fate with American power. America was alone this time around. The two volleys of Tomahawk missiles fired against Iraqi air-defense installations had to be launched from U.S. ships in the Persian Gulf and B-52 bombers that flew in from Guam. No one was fooled by the American response; no one believed that the foreign power would stay. U.S. officials wrote off that episode as an internal Kurdish fight, the doings of a fratricidal people. A subsequent air campaign—"fire and forget," skeptics dubbed it—gave the illusion of resolve and containment. But Clinton did not have his heart in that fight. He had put his finger to the wind and divined the mood in the land: there was no public tolerance for a major campaign against Saddam Hussein.

By the time the Bush administration stepped in, its leaders would find a checkered landscape. There was their old nemesis in Baghdad, wounded but not killed. There was a decade of Clintonianism that had invested its energy in the Israeli-Palestinian conflict but had paid the Persian Gulf scant attention. There was a pattern of half-hearted responses to terrorist attacks, pinpricks that fooled no one.

HAVING IT HIS WAY

IT WAS into this witch's brew that Arafat launched the second intifada last year. In a rare alignment, there had come Arafat's way a U.S. president keen to do his best and an Israeli soldier-statesman eager to grant the Palestinian leader all the Israeli body politic could yield—and then some. Arafat turned away from what was offered and headed straight back into his people's familiar history: the maximalism, the inability to read what can and cannot be had in a world of nations. He would wait for the "Arab street" to rise up in rebellion and force Pax Americana to redeem his claims. He would again let play on his people the old dream that they could have it all, from the river to the sea. He must know better, he must know the scales of power, it is reasonable to presume. But there still lurks in the Palestinian and Arab imagination a view, depicted by the Moroccan historian Abdallah Laroui, that "on a certain day, everything would be obliterated and instantaneously reconstructed and the new inhabitants would leave, as if by magic, the land they had despoiled." Arafat knew the power of this redemptive idea. He must have reasoned that it is safer to ride that idea, and that there will always be another day and another offer.

For all the fury of this second intifada, a supreme irony hangs over Palestinian history. In the early 1990s, the Palestinians had nothing to lose. Pariahs in the Arab councils of power, they made their best historical decision—the peace of Oslo—only when they broke with the maximalism of their political tradition. It was then that they crossed from Arab politics into internal Israeli politics and, courtesy of Israel, into the orbit of Pax Americana. Their recent return into inter-Arab politics was the resumption of an old, failed history.

Better the fire of an insurrection than the risks of reconciling his people to a peace he had not prepared them for: this was Arafat's way. This is why he spurned the offer at Camp David in the summer of 2000. "Yasir Arafat rode home on a white horse" from Camp David, said one of his aides, Nabil Shaath. He had shown that he "still cared about Jerusalem and the refugees." He had stood up, so Shaath said, to the combined pressure of the Americans and the Israelis. A creature of his time and his world, Arafat had come into his own amid the recriminations that followed the Arab defeat in 1948. Palestine had become an Arab shame, and the hunt for demons and sacrificial lambs would shape Arab politics for many years.

A temporizer and a trimmer, Arafat did not have it in him to tell the 1948 refugees in Lebanon, Syria, and Jordan that they were no more likely to find political satisfaction than were the Jews of Alexandria, Fez, Baghdad, and Beirut who were banished from Arab lands following Israel's statehood. He lit the fuse of this second intifada in the hope that others would put out the flame. He had become a player in Israeli politics, and there came to him this peculiar satisfaction that he could topple Israeli prime ministers, wait them out, and force an outside diplomatic intervention that would tip the scales in his favor. He could not give his people a decent public order and employ and train the young, but he could launch a war in the streets that would break Israel's economic momentum and rob it of the normalcy brought by the peace of Oslo.

Arafat had waited for rain, but on September 11, 2001, there had come the floods. "This is a new kind of war, a new kind of battlefield, and the United States will need the help of Arab and Muslim countries," chief Palestinian negotiator Saeb Erekat announced. The Palestinian issue, he added, was "certainly one of the reasons" for the attacks against the United States. An American-led brigade against terrorism was being assembled.

America was set to embark on another expedition into Arab-Muslim domains, and Arafat fell back on the old consolation that Arab assets would be traded on his people's behalf. A dowry would have to be offered to the Arab participants in this brigade: a U.S.-imposed settlement of the Israeli-Palestinian conflict. A cover would be needed for Arab regimes nervous about riding with the foreigner's posse, and it stood to reason that Arafat would claim that he could provide that kind of cover.

The terror that hit America sprang from entirely different sources. The plotters had been in American flight schools long before the "suicide martyrs" and the "children of the stones" had answered Arafat's call for an intifada. But the Palestinian leader and his lieutenants eagerly claimed that the fire raging in their midst had inspired the anti-American terror. A decade earlier, the Palestinians had hailed Saddam Hussein's bid for primacy in the Persian Gulf. Nonetheless, they had been given a claim on the peace—a role at the Madrid Conference of October 1991 and a solicitous U.S. policy. American diplomacy had arrived in the nick of time; the first intifada had burned out and degenerated into a hunt for demons and "collaborators." A similar fate lies in wait for the second intifada. It is reasonable to assume that Arafat expects rescue of a similar kind from the new American drive into Arab and Muslim lands.

No veto over national policies there will be given to Arafat. The states will cut their own deals. In the best of worlds, Pax Americana is doomed to a measure of solitude in the Middle East. This time around, the American predicament is particularly acute. Deep down, the Arab regimes feel that the threat of political Islam to their own turfs has been checked, and that no good can come out of an explicit public alliance with an American campaign in their midst. Foreign powers come and go, and there is very little protection they can provide against the wrath of an angry crowd. It is a peculiarity of the Arab-Islamic political culture that a ruler's authoritarianism is more permissible than his identification with Western powers—think of the fates of Sadat and of the Pahlavis of Iran.

Ride with the foreigners at your own risk, the region's history has taught. Syria's dictator, Hafiz al-Assad, died a natural death at a ripe old age, and his life could be seen as a kind of success. He never set foot on American soil and had stayed within his world. In contrast, the flamboyant Sadat courted foreign countries and came to a solitary, cruel end; his land barely grieved for him. A foreign power that stands sentry in that world cannot spare its local allies the retribution of those who brand them "collaborators" and betrayers of the faith. A coalition is in the offing, America has come calling, urging the region's rulers to "choose sides." What these rulers truly dread has come to pass: they might have to make fateful choices under the gaze of populations in the throes of a malignant anti-Americanism. The ways of that world being what they are, the United States will get more cooperation from the ministers of interior and the secret services than it will from the foreign ministers and the diplomatic interlocutors. There will be allies in the shadows, but in broad daylight the rulers will mostly keep their distance. Pakistan's ruler, Pervez Musharraf, has made a brave choice. The rulers all around must be reading a good deal of their worries into his attempt to stay the course and keep his country intact.

A broad coalition may give America the comfort that it is not alone in the Muslim world. A strike against Afghanistan is the easiest of things—far away from the troubles in the Persian Gulf and Egypt, from the head of the trail in Arab lands. The Taliban are the Khmer Rouge of this era and thus easy to deal with. The frustrations to come lie in the more ambiguous and impenetrable realms of the Arab world. Those were not Afghans who flew into those towers of glass and steel and crashed into the Pentagon. They were from the Arab world, where anti-Americanism is fierce, where terror works with the hidden winks that men and women make at the perpetrators of the grimmest of deeds.

BRAVE OLD WORLD

"WHEN THOSE PLANES flew into those buildings, the luck of America ran out," Leon Wieseltier recently wrote in *The New Republic.* The 1990s were a lucky decade, a fool's paradise. But we had not arrived at the end of history, not by a long shot. Markets had not annulled historical passions, and a high-tech world's electronic age had not yet dawned. So in thwarted, resentful societies there was satisfaction on September 11 that the American bull run and the triumphalism that had awed the world had been battered, that there was soot and ruin in New York's streets. We know better now. Pax Americana is there to stay in the oil lands and in Israeli-Palestinian matters. No large-scale retreat from those zones of American primacy can be contemplated. American hegemony is sure to hold—and so, too, the resistance to it, the uneasy mix in those lands of the need for the foreigner's order, and the urge to lash out against it, to use it and rail against it all the same.

There is now the distinct thunder of war. The first war of the twenty-first century is to be fought not so far from where the last inconclusive war of the twentieth century was waged against Iraq. The war will not be easy for America in those lands. The setting will test it in ways it has not been tested before. There will be regimes asking for indulgence for their own terrible fights against Islamists and for logistical support. There will be rulers offering the bait of secrets that their security services have accumulated through means at odds with American norms. Conversely, friends and sympathizers of terror will pass themselves off as constitutionalists and men and women of the "civil society." They will find shelter behind pluralist norms while aiding and abetting the forces of terror. There will be chameleons good at posing as America's friends but never turning up when needed. There will be one way of speaking to Americans, and another of letting one's population know that words are merely a pretense. There will step forth informers, hustlers of every shade, offering to guide the foreign power through the minefields and alleyways. America, which once held the world at a distance, will have to be willing to stick around eastern lands. It is both heartbreaking and ironic that so quintessentially American a figure as George W. Bush—a man who grew up in Midland, Texas, far removed from the complications of foreign places—must be the one to take his country on a journey into so alien, so difficult, a world.☻

Back to the Bazaar

Martin Indyk

THE POST—GULF WAR BARGAIN

A DECADE AGO, the United States faced a defining moment in the Middle East. It had just deployed overwhelming force to liberate Kuwait and destroy Iraq's offensive capabilities. The outcome of the Gulf War, combined with the collapse of the Soviet Union, had left the United States in an unprecedented position of dominance in the region. Washington was debating what to do with this newfound and unchallenged influence. With the rapid collapse of the Taliban regime in Afghanistan, the United States finds itself again at a crucial point of decision in the Middle East. But this time it has had little opportunity to ponder what to do. As Washington scrambles to define a policy for "phase two" of the campaign against terror, policymakers should look back to how the United States fared the last time it had such an opening.

At the end of the Gulf War, some idealists argued that it was time to spread democracy to a part of the world that knew little of it. They suggested starting with Iraq, using U.S. military might to topple Saddam Hussein and install a democratic regime, as had been done in Germany and Japan after World War II. And they questioned the wisdom of reinstalling the emir in liberated Kuwait, advocating instead that the United States should bring democracy to the sheikhdoms of the Persian Gulf.

MARTIN INDYK is Senior Fellow at the Brookings Institution. He served as Special Assistant to the President and Senior Director for Near East and South Asia on the staff of the National Security Council in 1993–95, as Assistant Secretary of State for Near East Affairs in 1997–2000, and as U.S. Ambassador to Israel in 1995–97 and 2000–2001.

Martin Indyk

These ideas got short shrift at the time. President George H.W. Bush strongly preferred the regional status quo, and America's Arab allies, determined to return to business as usual, were quick to reinforce his instinct. The Saudi rulers, for example, had come to understand how dangerous talk of democracy was for their own grip on power when Saudi women spontaneously expressed their desire for greater freedom by doing the hitherto unthinkable: driving themselves up and down the streets of Riyadh.

Even while the Iraq crisis was raging, these Arab allies had anticipated the idealistic U.S. impulses and had found a way to deflect them. They extracted from the president and his secretary of state, James Baker, a promise that after the war the United States would focus on solving the Arab-Israeli conflict. Sure enough, Washington obliged, leaving them alone to reestablish the old order in their troubled societies.

In October 1991, the Bush administration successfully used America's newfound regional dominance to convene the Madrid Middle East Peace Conference, which—for the first time in history—launched direct peace negotiations between Israel and all its Arab neighbors. And in June 1992, sensing the change in the local environment, Israelis went to the polls and delivered a mandate to Yitzhak Rabin to pursue peace. Thus, when President Bill Clinton assumed office in January 1993, he inherited an ongoing peace process, one that held out the promise of agreements on all fronts in short order.

Nevertheless, the new Democratic administration had come to Washington eager to promote democracy abroad. So the officials responsible for the task—particularly Morton Halperin on the staff of the National Security Council and John Shattuck in the State Department's Bureau of Democracy, Human Rights, and Labor—asked why the Middle East should be exempt. But those with responsibility for the Middle East (myself included) put forward a more powerful argument in favor of focusing on peacemaking rather than democratization.

Our case was straightforward. There was a window of opportunity to negotiate a comprehensive peace in the Middle East. If the negotiations were successful, that outcome would have a profound effect on the region, as leaders would no longer be able to use the excuse of conflict with Israel to delay political and economic reforms at home. Once peace was established, moreover, resources previously devoted to war could be freed up for reform. In the meantime, the United States could not afford the destabilizing impact that pressure for reform would generate in deeply traditional and repressed societies. Pushing hard for political change might not only disrupt the effort to promote peace but could also work against vital U.S. interests: stability in the oil-rich Persian Gulf and in strategically critical Egypt. The United States should therefore focus its energies on peacemaking, while containing the radical opponents of peace (Iraq, Iran, and Libya) and leaving friendly Arab regimes to deal with their internal problems as they saw fit.

This argument prevailed, and on its basis the Clinton administration fashioned a bargain with America's Arab allies that held, more or less, until September 11, 2001. Moderate Arab states would provide the U.S. military with access to bases and facilities to help contain the "rogues" and would support Washington's efforts to resolve the Arab-Israeli conflict; in return, Washington would not exert significant pressure for domestic change.

A MARRIAGE OF CONVENIENCE

THE UNITED STATES did not ignore political reform entirely; it just tinkered with it on the margins. The Clinton administration supported the right of women to vote in Qatar, Oman, and Kuwait (in the case of Kuwait, legislation granting that right was defeated by Islamic fundamentalists). It urged the Algerian regime, which was battling Islamist militants, to open some political space for its people and engage Islamist fundamentalists in dialogue (much to the chagrin of the French, who were more directly affected by instability in Algeria). It supported successful efforts by the kings of Morocco and Jordan to co-opt their political oppositions into government and parliament. And it made a significant effort to support democratic reforms in Yemen in the hope that, over time, change there might spur similar reforms in the rest of the Arabian Peninsula. But when it came to the mainstays of U.S. interest in the Arab world, Egypt and Saudi Arabia, Washington left well enough alone.

The administration was particularly worried that the Algerian malady might spread to Egypt. President Hosni Mubarak's government had become, to use Shakespeare's words, "weary, stale, flat, and unprofitable"—except, of course, for those lucky enough to be associated with it. Mubarak was confronting a particularly vicious form of Islamist militancy, promoted by the Gamayat Islamiya and the Egyptian Islamic Jihad, which were using murder and assassination to try to bring down the regime. In these circumstances, Washington decided to stand by Mubarak while he brutally suppressed his extremist opponents. There were occasional expressions of concern at human rights abuses cautiously documented by the State Department, but the Egyptians were far more sensitive to even this mild criticism than the administration expected them to be.

A high-level initiative, led by Vice President Al Gore, tried to get Mubarak to reform, privatize, and deregulate the Egyptian economy, in the belief that successful liberalization and modernization would have a profound demonstration effect on the rest of the Arab world and help Mubarak meet the basic needs of his people. But the Gore-Mubarak Commission was very much a partnership in which the United States provided encouragement but let the Egyptians dictate the pace.

In the Saudi case, the Clinton administration indulged Riyadh's penchant for buying off trouble as long as the regime also paid its huge arms bills, purchased Boeing aircraft, kept the price of oil within reasonable bounds, and allowed the United States to use Saudi air bases to enforce the southern no-fly zone over Iraq and launch occasional military strikes to contain Saddam Hussein.

Under pressure from Congress, the State Department occasionally and delicately raised concerns about religious freedom. But it never mentioned the "d" word. It watched the Saudi regime lock up or deport its opposition. When 19 American soldiers were killed in the terrorist bombing of the Khobar Towers in 1996, the United States accommodated the Saudis by moving the bulk of U.S. forces out into the desert, where they would be unseen and less easily targeted. (Typical of the bargain, the Saudis paid the bill for the move.) The administration tussled with the Saudi government to get access to the perpetrators, but the attempt succeeded only after the Saudis had reached a modus vivendi with the Iranian government and were confident that the trail of evidence would not be adequate to justify U.S. retaliation against Tehran. And perhaps most significant, in retrospect, the administration tolerated Saudi Arabia's relationship with the Taliban regime in Afghanistan, hoping that the United States could use Saudi influence to get the Taliban to expel Osama bin Laden.

Overall, the policy toward Egypt and Saudi Arabia seemed successful. Mubarak overcame the threat of Islamist extremism and stabilized his regime. His government was able to show modest achievements from the U.S.-sponsored economic reform. Although the United States had some tense moments with the Saudis, the relationship served the interests of both sides. Despite occasional protestations to the contrary for the benefit of their respective publics, both the Egyptian and the Saudi regimes were comfortable with the containment of Saddam Hussein and willing to assist the United States quietly in its use of force to maintain that containment. Both balked when it came to providing support for an effort to remove him, but since the United States had little confidence in that endeavor itself, their demurrals did not pose a significant problem.

The disillusionment, to the extent there was any, came from the failure of both Egypt and Saudi Arabia to play any significantly helpful role in the Arab-Israeli peace process, which the United States had launched partly at their behest. The Saudis provided modest financial assistance to the Palestinians but otherwise kept their distance; the Egyptians were usually prepared to endorse Palestinian Authority leader Yasir Arafat's decisions but rarely prepared to press him, and Cairo occasionally even opposed Washington's efforts, especially when it came to promoting Israel's regional integration. At the critical moment in November 2000 when Clinton put forward U.S. parameters for resolving the Israeli-Palestinian conflict, both the Saudis and the Egyptians privately signaled their acquiescence but failed to provide any demonstrable support for the deal.

In spite of these shortcomings, however, Washington, Cairo, and Riyadh had a workable deal. Their bargain worked because they had a common interest in maintaining the stability of the status quo.

THE PROBLEMS UNDER THE RUG

AND THEN came September 11—a direct attack on the United States killing around 3,000 people, a day of infamy that should have changed everything. Americans have started to ask questions: How was it that the leaders of al Qaeda, the organization that perpetrated the attacks, were a Saudi and an Egyptian? And why did so many of the hijackers come from Saudi Arabia and Egypt, America's two closest Arab allies? If the United States is going to uproot the terrorists, as President George W. Bush insists, does it not also need to, in the words of one U.S. official, "dry up" the Egyptian and Saudi "swamps" that bred them?

These questions are indicative of the new understanding Americans are developing of what happened while their government was busy taking Egyptian and Saudi advice and focusing on peacemaking in the Middle East. The effective suppression of the Islamist opposition in Egypt and Saudi Arabia forced the extremists first to seek refuge and then to set up operations outside the region, in Africa, Asia, Europe, and the United States. The al Qaeda network established by bin Laden (a Saudi) and his associate Ayman al-Zawahiri (an Egyptian) wanted to overthrow the Saudi and Egyptian regimes, but with U.S. support these governments had become hardened targets. So al Qaeda made a strategic decision to strike at their patron, the more powerful but also more vulnerable United States.

The Saudis had protected themselves by co-opting and accommodating the Islamist extremists in their midst, a move they felt was necessary in the uncertain aftermath of the Gulf War. Since Saddam Hussein remained in power, weakened but still capable of lashing out and intent on revenge, the Saudis could not afford to send their American protector packing. Instead, they found a way to provide the United States with the access it needed to protect Saudi Arabia while keeping the American profile as low as possible. They were not oblivious to the bonanza that a U.S. military presence in the Islamic holy land created for their internal critics. And once Crown Prince Abdullah assumed the regency in 1996, the ruling family set about the determined business of buying off its opposition.

Back to the Bazaar

One mainstay of Abdullah's policy was rapprochement with Iran, which required burying any connection between the Khobar bombing and Ayatollah Khomeini's regime. Less noticed by the administration, because it seemed less important to U.S. interests, was a new development in the partnership that had long existed between the House of Saud and the Wahhabi religious sect, which practiced a puritanical and intolerant form of Islam. This partnership had already resulted in the ceding of control over social, religious, and educational affairs to the Wahhabis in return for the burnishing of the Islamic legitimacy of the royal family. The vulnerabilities exposed by the Gulf War, however, created a greater need for shoring up Wahhabi support. The regime accordingly financed the export of Wahhabism through the building of hundreds of mosques and *madrassas* (religious schools) abroad. The activity was particularly intense in areas affected by the collapse of the Soviet Union—the Balkans, Central Asia, Afghanistan, and Pakistan—where the Saudis engaged in competition with Iranian mullahs for the hearts and minds of local Muslim populations. A public-private partnership was also created in which rich Saudi families would help to fund the enterprise.

While Saudi export of Wahhabism was proceeding apace, the charitable organizations established to funnel the money were being subverted for other purposes. It is now clear that bin Laden, despite being stripped of his Saudi citizenship, was able to take advantage of this system to raise funds and establish his network. Saudi-backed institutions such as the International Islamic Relief Organization, the Muslim World League, and the Muwafaq Foundation were used as covers for financing al Qaeda's nefarious activities. And the Sunni fundamentalist Taliban regime in Afghanistan, providers of sanctuary to bin Laden and his cohort, also found itself the direct and indirect beneficiary of Saudi largess.

Egypt pursued a different but in the end equally damaging route. With its much larger population and with far fewer resources for purchasing the allegiance of its disaffected, the Mubarak government confronted its violent and ruthless Islamist opposition with brute force. The resulting conflict cost more than 1,200 lives between 1992 and 1997. Given the terrorist tactics of the Islamist militants, the regime's response appeared the only answer. Along the way, however,

Cairo also suppressed legitimate dissent, effectively reducing the already limited space allowed for civil society. The incarceration of Saad Edin Ibrahim, a distinguished Egyptian sociologist who criticized the regime for election irregularities, is a celebrated case in point. The regime also tried to introduce a law placing all nongovernmental organizations under strict government control. Having defeated its opponents through incarceration or exile, moreover, and having deflected the United States by insisting it focus on Arab-Israeli peacemaking, the Mubarak government also succeeded in deflecting criticism away from itself. An anti-American consensus was created between Islamist fundamentalists on the right, who regarded Americans as infidels; pan-Arab nationalists on the left, who viewed Americans as imperialists; and the regime itself, which found it convenient for the Egyptian intellectual class to criticize the United States and Israel rather than its own government's shortcomings.

In retrospect, the September 11 attacks and the hatred they revealed toward America in the Islamic world can be seen as the logical consequence of these trends. The question now, therefore, is not whether the United States needs to renegotiate the bargain it struck in the 1990s with the governments of Egypt and Saudi Arabia; the death of so many Americans demands such a reappraisal. Instead we should look to a new deal. What new bargain can and should be struck with Arab allies with whom the United States shares common strategic interests but whose policies are compromising U.S. national security?

A POSTNUPTIAL AGREEMENT?

AMERICA'S ARAB ALLIES have been quick to register their requirements for participating in the coalition against terrorism: no Israeli participation, no attacks on any Arab country (including Iraq), and a new initiative to solve the Israeli-Palestinian problem. By and large the Bush administration has been responsive to these requirements. Israel's participation—providing quiet intelligence cooperation, training for special forces, and advice on homeland defense—has been as low-key as the Arabs' own. Washington's hot contest over whether to use this crisis as justification for launching a war against Iraq is apt to be deferred until business in Afghanistan is successfully concluded. And, succumbing to intense pressure from Saudi Arabia and Egypt, the president has overcome his skepticism and allowed Secretary of State Colin Powell to launch a new initiative to stop the violence of the renewed Palestinian intifada, the necessary precursor to a more robust effort to resolve the Palestinian problem.

The United States, however, has been slower to determine and register its own needs. The short-term requirement is clear enough: overt support for the war on terror. This demand is not yet an issue of military backing. The war in Afghanistan has required only low-profile intelligence, logistical, and communications support from U.S. partners in the Middle East, which the Egyptians and the Saudis have been willing to provide. The crunch will come later, if the United States decides to go after Saddam, since that effort cannot succeed without access to Saudi and Egyptian facilities. America's Arab allies are prepared to provide tacit support for a war in Afghanistan but are no longer willing to provide active military support for a war against an Arab country. Indeed, absent clear evidence of Iraqi involvement in the September 11 or anthrax attacks, if Washington judges a war on Iraq as necessary to the new bargain, there is unlikely to be any deal at all.

Yet if Egypt and Saudi Arabia will not back a U.S. military campaign to remove Saddam from power, Washington should at least insist that they actively join in the effort to shut down Middle Eastern safe havens for terrorists. As the United States turns its focus to other states that allow terrorists to operate from their territory, it will need its Arab friends to make clear to Iran, Iraq, Syria, and Lebanon that they will be on their own in the Arab world and the international community if they continue to provide succor for terrorists. In the 1990s, Saudi Arabia was able to convince Iran to end its support for terrorism and subversion in the Arabian Peninsula; it should now use the same powers of persuasion on all the state sponsors of terrorism in its neighborhood. Many of those governments will argue that terrorism is justified because it is aimed at Israelis. But President Bush answered that argument decisively when he addressed the U.N. General Assembly in November, asserting that "no national aspiration, no remembered wrong can ever justify the deliberate murder of the innocent." At a time when America's Arab friends are expecting the United States to promote Arab-Israeli peace, the

United States will need them to actively oppose the Middle Eastern terrorism that has done so much in the past to impede its attainment.

Drying up the sources of funding for al Qaeda is also an urgent priority. The United States must insist that Saudi Arabia undertake a complete overhaul of public and private Saudi funding for charitable organizations and institute new regulations for monitoring the flow of funds.

One of the most important requirements will come in the battle for the hearts and minds of Muslims around the world. Here Washington needs the Egyptian and Saudi governments, as the most influential players in the Arab and Islamic worlds, to take the lead in legitimizing its assertion that it is not at war with Islam. The United States also needs its Arab allies to make the case to their own people and to Muslims everywhere that U.S. objectives are justified because the terrorists have defamed Islam and done great damage to the Islamic cause. Washington has to persuade Cairo and Riyadh to lead public opinion through a sustained campaign in their government-controlled media and their government-funded mosques. These governments' essential silence in these matters to date conveys the impression that they are afraid of public opinion. Yet the prevailing calm in their streets, in the face of an intense U.S. bombing campaign in Afghanistan, indicates that the Egyptian and Saudi regimes have less to fear than they imagined. They should at least start to encourage those thin, small voices in their media that are holding a mirror to their own societies rather than joining the default chorus that avoids responsibility by blaming the United States.

Calming the situation in the West Bank and Gaza will also help to remove the excuse that the Egyptian and Saudi governments use to avoid taking stands in defense of the United States. Powell's initiative, launched on November 19, presented the right mix: one part broad vision of an eventual two-state solution, and four parts specific steps involving stopping the violence, arresting terrorists, ending the Palestinian incitement, and ceasing settlement activity. Dispatching envoys to the region to sustain the initiative, as Washington has done, is also the only effective way to test whether September 11 has changed the calculations of Chairman Arafat and Israeli Prime Minister Ariel Sharon enough to end the intifada and resume meaningful negotiations.

Back to the Bazaar

But now that the United States has allowed Saudi Arabia and Egypt to make their bids for a new bargain, this time Washington must be much more insistent that these governments reciprocate. They must partner U.S. efforts to resolve the Palestinian problem. It is unacceptable that at a time when Washington is insisting that the Palestinian Authority end its anti-Israel incitement campaign, Cairo and Riyadh should do nothing to counter the vitriolic anti-semitism in their media and the shameful efforts to legitimize terrorist attacks against civilians because they happen to be Israelis. It is also unacceptable, given the genesis of this new U.S. initiative, that the Saudi and Egyptian governments should sit on the sidelines while the United States tries to broker an agreement. They will need to be public advocates of fair and reasonable compromises on the critical issues of Jerusalem and refugees. And, in the Saudi case, Washington should not heed Riyadh's insistence on Israeli and U.S. recognition of a Palestinian state unless the Saudis are willing to reciprocate by extending their own recognition to Israel.

LET'S MAKE A DEAL

THE LONGER-TERM U.S. requirements for a new bargain are even more problematic. If the United States is to "dry up the swamp" that generated the al Qaeda terrorist phenomenon, it is going to have to confront the dilemma of political change in the Arab world. In the past, recognizing that the dynamics of change in traditional societies could be deeply destabilizing, Washington posed the choice as one "between corruption and chaos." It opted to back corrupt governments because it feared that the alternative would be worse for vital U.S. interests. In the case of Iran, the United States backed the shah for fear of the alternative. In the end it got the alternative anyway. The theocratic regime of ayatollahs that replaced the shah was far worse, and U.S. support for the shah contributed to the profound anti-American manifestations of the Iranian Revolution. It was the worst of all worlds.

In the Egyptian and Saudi cases the dilemma has now been exacerbated. The United States backed their regimes and they begat al Qaeda. But insisting on political reform in Cairo and Riyadh could help bin Laden achieve his ultimate objective: toppling these regimes even after he has gone. That outcome would be the ultimate irony. Whatever the shortcomings of these regimes, fundamentalist alternatives are bound to be worse for the Egyptian and Saudi people, as they were for Iran and Afghanistan. And revolution in Saudi Arabia and Egypt could have a devastating impact on vital U.S. interests in the Middle East. Yet if they do not change their ways, over time these regimes could fall anyway, and in the meantime their failings may continue to generate unacceptable threats to U.S. national security.

The way out is to develop a middle path, working with the Egyptian and Saudi governments to promote political and economic reform—even if doing so requires them to loosen some controls and take some risks. They have to be persuaded that opening political space for the encouragement of civil society in their countries can help to legitimize their regimes rather than destabilize them. The Saudis and the Egyptians will also need to be encouraged to develop a more tolerant model of Islam, one more reconciled to modernity, as an alternative to the hatred and xenophobia now propagated through school and mosque. And they will have be prodded into undertaking economic reforms that can provide meaningful employment and the hope of a better future for their young people, who now make up the majority in these countries.

All of this, of course, is much easier said than done. U.S. efforts to promote such an agenda would have met opposition even during easier times; in the midst of an Islamist confrontation with the United States, the resistance will be stiffer yet. On the other hand, success in the war against al Qaeda and the Taliban will open a window of opportunity just as did success against Iraq during the Gulf War a decade ago. When this window opens, the United States will need to seize the moment and put its demands on the table, so it should be formulating them now. In this regard, one question to examine is whether Islamic states that have embarked on political and economic reform can provide models for others to emulate. Jordan, for example, is a weak, resource-poor buffer state. Yet its ruling Hashemites have found a way to bring Islamic fundamentalists into the mainstream of political life even as the government vigorously pursues terrorist cells within the country's borders, and to promote economic reform while maintaining their peace treaty with Israel. Similarly, Morocco's leadership has brought its political opposition into the government while embarking on social and economic reforms.

America's Egyptian and Saudi interlocutors will come to the postwar bargaining table with counter-demands. Just as they did after the Gulf War, they will do their best to deflect the United States by focusing attention on solving the Palestinian problem. The United States has its own reasons for making this issue a priority, but this time around pursuing Arab-Israeli peace needs to be part of the bargain and not a substitute for it. And in return, Washington will need Cairo and Riyadh to act as full partners in the peacemaking effort.

But beyond that, the United States will have to persuade the Egyptian and Saudi governments to attend to its short-term needs in the continuing war on terrorism and to begin working on their own long-term need to address more effectively their people's basic requirements for greater political and economic progress. Persuading Arab leaders to stop financing terrorism, promote tolerance in their societies, and cooperate with the United States in shutting down terrorist safe havens in the Middle East are conditions that Washington must insist on—the failure to do so will have a direct impact on U.S. national security. Persuading them to undertake difficult political and economic reforms, however, could have a direct impact on their own security, which would make them more resistant to U.S. arguments.

Nevertheless, the United States can no longer afford to desist from this longer-term task. At a minimum, America's Arab friends must know that political and economic reform will be an integral part of the ongoing U.S. agenda with them—a constant issue in diplomatic exchanges, a subject for congressional scrutiny, and a component of U.S. assistance programs. Even if they start paying attention to these issues only to get Washington off their backs, they will create openings for the growth of civil society in their countries.

Merely listing the parameters of such a new deal with the leaders of the Arab world suggests how difficult and daunting the task of negotiating it will be. The main reason even to try, in fact, is simply because the United States has few alternatives. If it allows another return to business as usual, as it did after the Gulf War, it will sow the seeds of its own destruction in the Middle East—and that of its regional allies as well.❧

Trouble in the Kingdom

Eric Rouleau

AT SEA IN THE DESERT

CROWN PRINCE ABDULLAH cut an impressive figure when he arrived in Crawford, Texas, in late April to meet with President George W. Bush. The man who has ruled Saudi Arabia ever since his half brother, King Fahd, suffered a stroke in 1995, Abdullah managed to present himself as both firm and conciliatory, establishing a productive dialogue with the American president and improving a relationship that had been badly frayed by September 11 and the ongoing crisis in the Middle East. While pressuring Bush to take a more active role in the Arab-Israeli peace process, Abdullah also mollified the Americans by promising to keep Saudi oil flowing and by promoting his own groundbreaking solution to the conflict in the Middle East.

Abdullah's performance abroad, however, obscured the fact that the prince's power at home—and indeed, the health of his nation—has eroded significantly. A major crisis is now brewing in Saudi Arabia, and September's terrorist attacks—committed by 19 hijackers, 15 of whom were Saudi citizens—both highlighted and, in a way, aggravated the tensions in the kingdom. The intense violence in the Middle East has made matters even worse. The deterioration of the Arab-Israeli situation has started to threaten the very stability of the Saudi state in a way many Westerners, particularly Americans, had not anticipated. In particular, outsiders have underestimated the anger roused in the Saudi population by the suffering of the Palestinian people—and the fact that this suffering is blamed less on Is-

ERIC ROULEAU, a writer, was France's Ambassador to Tunisia from 1985 to 1986 and to Turkey from 1988 to 1992.

rael than on its American protector. Given the privileged nature of relations between Washington and Riyadh, this anger has also started to focus on the House of Saud itself.

Although Westerners may not have anticipated the current crisis, it came as no surprise to Abdullah. A month before September 11, the crown prince had already warned Bush about the rising danger, asking him to intervene in the Middle East to help bring about a "balanced" settlement of the Israeli-Palestinian conflict. According to his close aides, however, Abdullah's early oral and written messages to Bush were treated with skepticism in Washington, leading the prince, in an unprecedented gesture, to refuse an invitation to visit the White House.

It was his despair at Washington's refusal to get involved that led the crown prince to launch a bold peace initiative of his own in February, promising full normalization of relations between Israel and the entire Arab world in exchange for the implementation of the UN's resolutions on Palestine. The peace deal—extended directly "to the government and the people of Israel"—was clearer and more precise than any that had been formulated since the creation of the Jewish state. Coming at a time when most Arabs were outraged by the Israeli army's conduct in the occupied territories, Abdullah's offer was a risky move, capable of triggering violent protests at home and likely to be rejected by Israel. Yet Abdullah backed the proposal enthusiastically, even managing to twist the arms of several reluctant Arab governments to ensure its unanimous acceptance at the March 2002 Arab League summit.

Abdullah's moves represented more than just an attempt to defuse the time bomb of popular anger threatening all current Arab regimes. He also hoped to save his own government's privileged relationship with the United States—an alliance that has been critical to Saudi Arabia's security and one to which Abdullah therefore attaches great importance. But not many Saudis seem to agree with the prince's priorities. Since his peace initiative was first announced, the Saudi security forces have had to put down anti-American and anti-Israeli demonstrations in at least three cities—Riyadh, Al Jauf, and Dhahran—and liberal Saudi intellectuals have circulated a petition calling for the rupture of diplomatic ties with the United States and (following Iraq's example) an oil embargo. Even before these incidents, a number of Western diplomats had already concluded that Saudi Arabia was fast becoming one of the most anti-American countries in the Gulf. Unless the United States succeeds in restarting serious and credible Israeli-Palestinian (and Israeli-Syrian) negotiations, Abdullah may not be able to contain the groundswell of opposition rising up in his country. This opposition poses intense risks for both countries; indeed, if not controlled it could tear apart a strategic alliance that has lasted since World War II.

BEYOND BELIEF

THE ONE ISSUE that angers the Saudis the most is Israel's treatment of the Palestinians, whom Saudis view as engaged in a legitimate independence struggle against a brutal—and American-backed—colonial oppressor. Another strong grievance, however, is the presence of American bases on Arabian soil. Despite official denials, the U.S. troops, who have been in Saudi Arabia ever since the Persian Gulf War, are highly unpopular. In keeping with strict government orders, the issue is not raised in the media or in public. In private, however, many Saudis complain that they consider it a form of occupation—at best humiliating, since the regime should not have to rely on foreign protection, and at worst intolerable, since the U.S. bases may eventually become a staging ground for military operations against fellow Muslim countries such as Iraq. The U.S. presence undermines the government's legitimacy as well; "Ever since the Gulf War of 1991," complains Prince Nayef, minister of the interior and brother of King Fahd, "we are perceived in the Arab world as a pawn of the United States."

More generally, however, Saudis also object to the entire thrust and tenor of Washington's foreign policy, which they see as arbitrary, unjust, and dismissive or contemptuous of Arab interests. Critics fault the United States for its unilateralism. "The arrogance of the United States is unacceptable," declared one young prince, speaking on condition of anonymity. "President Bush says that anyone who does not fully support the U.S. war plans is with the ter-

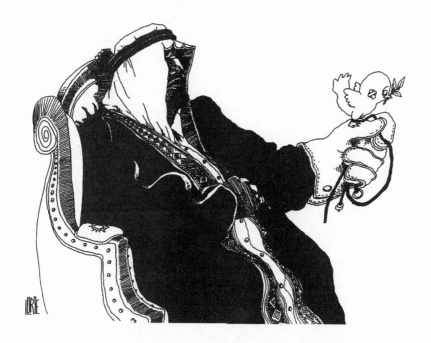

rorists," he remarked. "In other words, we are being asked to board a train without being told where it is going, what route it will follow, or how long the journey will take. And we're told not to ask questions, which are considered inappropriate."

Not only do Saudis resent being told what to do, they were also profoundly shocked by the widespread skepticism displayed in the U.S. media about the kingdom's determination to fight terrorism after September's attacks. After all, as Prince Nayef has indignantly argued, al Qaeda is even more dangerous to Saudi Arabia than it is to the United States. America will never suffer anything more than physical attacks, he points out, which, however devastating and costly they may be, will not undermine the state itself. "For us, on the other hand, the threat is also—and especially—ideological and political, since [Osama] bin Laden accuses the royal family of betraying Islam and of being an accomplice of the United States." To prove his good faith, Prince Nayef then listed the antiterrorist measures his country adopted well before September 11, which included the establishment of tight coordination with Western and Arab intelligence agencies, the arrests of scores of extremists, and the execution of those found guilty of anti-American attacks on Saudi soil.

Yet bin Laden remains widely popular in Saudi Arabia today—not for his crimes, but because of the population's reflexive anti-Americanism. Contrary to widespread opinion in the West, the Saudis—like the citizens of the other Gulf countries—do not attribute to bin Laden any Islamic legitimacy or authority. But even though his actions may be seen as contrary to the precepts of Islam, al Qaeda's founder is considered a hero for having challenged the United States by striking two key symbols of its power: the World Trade Center and the Pentagon. It is nationalism, not Islam, that remains the dominant ideology in Arabia today, and this explains bin Laden's ongoing appeal.

Most Saudis actually believe that Islamic radicalism, such as that which bin Laden espouses, is foreign to both their religion and their traditions. One of the rare intellectuals who openly acknowledges the kingdom's responsibility for the spread of political extremism is Askar Enazy, a professor of international relations with university degrees from the United States, Canada, the United Kingdom, and Russia. He reproaches the Saudi leaders—as well as the American government—for having unintentionally allowed this "cancer" to spread.

Threatened by the Arab nationalism that led to the overthrow of governments elsewhere in the region in the 1950s and 1960s, Saudi Arabia granted political asylum to thousands of members of the Muslim Brotherhood who were fleeing repression in Egypt, Syria, and Iraq. These men brought with them a doctrine of political Islam formulated by the movement's founder, Hassan al Banna, and developed by the theoretician of jihad, Sayed Qutb, who was executed in 1966 by Egyptian President Gamal Abdel Nasser. And they soon came to exert vast influence in Saudi Arabia. Employed as imams in mosques, as instructors and professors in schools and universities, and as senior officials in the ministry of education, members of the Muslim Brotherhood designed school textbooks and syllabuses and published works interpreting the Koran along the strict guidelines of their beliefs. In the process, they won numerous local disciples, including many within the Saudi clergy.

Until the arrival of the Muslim Brotherhood, Wahhabi Islam, the official state religion in Saudi Arabia, had been essentially apolitical, concerning itself mainly with puritanism in morals, the observance of proper dress, and correct religious practices per se. Under the impact of the new arrivals, however, part of the Saudi clergy progressively became politicized—and began, for the first time, to challenge the House of Saud's temporal power.

The royal family, however, did not initially grasp this slow metamorphosis or the potential threat political Islam entailed. In fact, the government seemed to think it could control the movement. Riyadh thus launched an Islamization campaign throughout the Arab Islamic world in the early 1970s. Taking advantage of the windfall provided by the first oil boom, the Saudis funneled substantial revenues into financing Islamic movements abroad, building thousands of mosques, religious schools, and cultural centers, and sending contingents of imams and other missionaries to spread the good word. The goal was to fight atheism, communism, and secular pan-Arabism while at the same time extending Saudi influence in "brotherly countries." These objectives also happened to coincide perfectly with U.S. concerns during the Cold War; as a result, the Islamists were generally considered the natural allies of the West until the early 1990s.

The United States, in fact, joined forces with Saudi Arabia and Pakistan to recruit, arm, finance, and train tens of thousands of mujahideen for the "Islamist International" that was assembled to help drive the Soviets from Afghanistan. One of these fighters, of course, just happened to be bin Laden, who was supported and encouraged at first by Saudi intelligence in cooperation with the CIA. The mutation of a freedom-fighter into a dangerous dissident began only with his return home after the Soviet defeat. Bin Laden was shocked by Riyadh's refusal in 1990 to let him organize new brigades of the mujahideen to drive the Iraqis out of Kuwait and to overthrow Saddam Hussein's secular regime; he became even more indignant when his government participated in Operation Desert Storm and subsequently leased military bases on Arabian soil—holy land—to the United States. This outrage finally brimmed over in 1991, when bin Laden turned his jihad against the United States and its allies.

Even then Saudi Arabia and the United States did not recognize the threat that political Islam posed; bin Laden's onslaught was seen as an isolated case. Washington and Riyadh continued to find the contribution of the "Arab Afghans"—the mujahideen who had cut their teeth fighting the Soviets in Afghanistan—useful in the struggle against Slavic hegemony elsewhere: in Bosnia, Kosovo, Chechnya, and Macedonia, as well as in the fight against the Marxist regime of South Yemen. Even the Taliban were considered potential allies at first. Their religious practices, inspired by Saudi Wahhabis, appeared innocently apolitical: the Afghan mullahs had been indoctrinated in religious schools set up in Pakistan using Saudi money and instructors, and the Taliban troops were trained, armed, and led by the Pakistani army and intelligence services. This degree of outside support, it was thought, would make them controllable. The Taliban, moreover, were seen as the enemy of the enemy of the West; after all, their opponents, the Northern Alliance, were supported by Iran and Russia.

"We recognized the Taliban regime only after America gave the green light," recounts one Saudi cabinet minister. "We shared the conviction that [Taliban leader Mullah Muhammad] Omar's followers were the only ones capable of restoring unity and civil peace in Afghanistan, which in fact turned out to be the case during the first two years of their rule." Washington did not ask Riyadh and Islamabad to break off relations with Kabul until after September 11.

The United States' ongoing indulgence of the Taliban can be explained by several factors. American envoys had begun secretly negotiating the extradition of bin Laden with Mullah Omar's representatives as early as 1997. An American oil firm, Unocal, also happened to be engaged in parallel talks to obtain permission to build a pipeline across Afghanistan linking Turkmenistan to Pakistan and the Arabian Sea. Zalmay Khalilzad, an Afghan-born American who is now Bush's special envoy to Kabul, actually worked as a consultant for Unocal in the late 1990s. And although he subsequently reversed his opinion, in 1996 he wrote an op-ed in *The Washington Post* urging the White House to recognize the Taliban government—which he argued was neither anti-American nor terrorist.

In light of Washington's pre–September 11 record on Afghanistan, it is no wonder Saudi officials are indignant when the American media now accuse them of being responsible for the growth of Islamic terrorism. The Saudis, after all, thought they were acting in line with American interests. Some of them, therefore, now question whether the U.S. intelligence community is trying to blame them for al Qaeda in order to deflect attention from its own failure. Other Saudis see a nefarious "Jewish lobby" at work, trying to use the situation to drive a wedge between Washington and Riyadh. Conspiracy theories aside, however, most Saudi elites remain determined to maintain the special relationship with the United States. Too many common interests, they explain, exist to risk breaking an alliance that has served both sides for six decades.

DOMESTIC DISTURBANCES

WHATEVER HAPPENS in the foreign policy domain, Saudi Arabia also now faces a serious domestic crisis that could destabilize the regime in the long run. "We live in a schizophrenic state," one prominent member of the royal family recently remarked. The expression, heard frequently in upper-class Saudi homes, is by no means an exaggeration. The foreign visitor arriving in Riyadh is immediately struck by the kingdom's modernity; by one of the most spacious airports in the world, luxurious and functional; by the wide, tree-lined boulevards of the capital, with elegant buildings, proud towers, American-style shopping centers, and cyber-cafés; and by the kingdom's computerized administration and businesses.

But there exists another Saudi Arabia, equally striking. This is the country that, since the demise of the Taliban, now bears the dubious distinction of being the most rigorous theocracy in the Islamic world. (One runner-up, the emirate of Qatar, also follows Wahhabi Islam but allows the consumption of alcoholic beverages in public places, like most of the other Gulf states.) In this Saudi Arabia, the Koran serves as the constitution and is interpreted as prohibiting such things as movie houses, theaters, discotheques, and concerts. Fully half of the population—namely, Saudi women—are banned from public spaces unless they cloak themselves in black from head to toe. Women are also treated as legal minors: instead of having her own individual identity card or passport, for example, a Saudi woman is listed on the documents of her male guardian (although starting this year, women can now obtain their own cards, but only at their guardians' request and with their guarantee). A Saudi woman cannot undertake the most routine administrative procedure, open a bank account, purchase property, work, or travel without the express approval of her guardian. Nor are women in Saudi Arabia allowed to drive. Officially, they can work only in two fields: education and medicine, and even there they must be segregated from their male colleagues. As a result of such strictures, tens of thousands of female university graduates do not work outside their homes. The mingling of the sexes is likewise forbidden in schools; universities require male professors teaching women's classes to give their lectures through a closed-circuit one-way television system, ensuring that the lecturers cannot see their students.

Not only women suffer under this system. At least 65 percent of the Saudi population is now under 25 years of age, and the frustrations felt by these youngsters are enormous. The kingdom's puritanical rules prevent young people from mixing with the opposite sex or enjoying the kinds of pastimes taken for granted elsewhere. Without meaningful outlets for their energy or ways to spend spare time, increasing numbers are turning to the illicit consumption of alcohol and drugs. They are also turning to satellite television and to the Internet, which serve only to broaden their horizons and give them a window on the modern world—making their restrictions all the more onerous and helping ensure that their aspirations differ markedly from those of their elders.

Saudi Arabia's educational system also prevents many young men from finding productive jobs. The Saudi media are good at pointing out that local schools have churned out a mediocre work force ill adapted to the needs of modern corporations. But they fail to mention a salient explanation for this problem: 30 to 40 percent of the course hours in schools are devoted to studying scripture. The teaching of non-Islamic philosophy, meanwhile, is banned. As a result, Saudi university graduates end up more qualified to analyze holy texts than to work as engineers, architects, computer specialists, or managers. And this in turn means that many heads of Saudi companies prefer to employ foreigners rather than locals; in fact, a full two-thirds of the work force is now foreign. Expatriates are considered more competent than Saudis, and cheaper: they can be paid four to five times less than citizens. These factors together contribute to an unemployment rate of about 30 percent among Saudi men and 95 percent for women. These figures, moreover, are constantly rising because of a population growth rate that is among the highest in the world (more than three percent annually, birth control being seen as contrary to Islam), and because of a general failure of job creation. "We are the only country in the world that imports the unemployed from other countries in order to swell the ranks of the unemployed among its own people," quips Enazy.

The resulting social tensions have begun to take various forms. Among them has been a significant drop in marriage rates. Unable to afford the traditional dowry, many young Saudi men are now doomed to a prolonged celibacy. At the same time, growing numbers of young women are refusing to marry men chosen for them by their families, men whom their would-be brides are not allowed to meet before their wedding night. As a result, an estimated two-thirds of Saudi women now between 16 and 30 years of age cannot, or will not, marry.

Aggravating Saudi Arabia's general social malaise are severe economic problems. Business leaders who lack connections to the royal family and the exceptional privileges these bring must struggle in an environment that discourages commerce. Potential lenders and investors are stymied by obstacles such as an archaic judicial system based on the *shari`a* (Islamic law) and applied by religious courts; laws forbidding the establishment of local insurance companies on the grounds that they practice "usury," forbidden by Islam; and the nontransparency of state accounts. Saudi citizens keep much of their money abroad; these foreign investments, mainly in the United States, are estimated by Western bankers to total anywhere from $700 billion to a trillion dollars. Saudis have not brought this money home, not even since the September 11 attacks. But as a result, there is not enough money for local investment, and the kingdom's private sector generates only a third of GDP.

In the past, the Saudi state was able to use oil money to compensate for the shortcomings of private enterprise. But this is no longer possible; in fact, contrary to widespread perceptions abroad, Saudi Arabia, which should be the richest nation in the Gulf, is now far worse off than many of its neighbors. The Saudi budget has run a deficit ever since the vast outlays of the Gulf War a decade ago. That war cost the kingdom more than $60 billion, mostly to cover the United States' military outlay during the operation. Since then, Riyadh has spent tens of billions of additional dollars, often uselessly, on American weaponry. Thanks to such crushing expenditures, the kingdom now has the highest indebtedness in the Gulf: $171 billion in domestic loans and $35 billion in foreign credits, or 107 percent of the country's GDP. Unstable oil revenues are hardly sufficient to repay this debt or even to compensate state employees (who number more than a million); government salaries have already been frozen for years.

Inevitably, the population overall has become poorer: per capita income plunged from $28,600 in 1981 (equivalent to that of the United States the same year) to $6,800 last year. By comparison, the average per capita revenue in Abu Dhabi is $36,000, and in Qatar it is $26,000. To redress the situation, Crown Prince Abdullah has set two general goals: to modernize the state apparatus, and to liberalize the economy. To attract foreign capital, critically important for relaunching productive enterprises, generous incentives are being offered to potential investors. Prince Abdullah has also appointed a particularly enlightened and dynamic man, Prince Abdullah bin Faisal bin Turki, to head the Saudi Arabian General Investment Authority, and the latter prince has managed in one year to increase investments by more than $10 billion. The opening of the gas sector to foreign companies—an unprecedented step since the nationalization of the Arabian American Oil Company (Aramco) in 1976—is also expected to bring in an additional $30 billion within ten years. And a vast privatization program, if ever implemented, should inject still more into the economy. Draft legislation is being prepared to legalize insurance companies, to introduce the right to a defense in the courts, to establish labor regulations, and to create a human rights organization—all positive signs.

TOO LITTLE, TOO LATE?

NOT EVERYONE has been impressed by the recent initiatives, however. Prince Talal, for example—another of King Fahd's half brothers, and a man long known as one of the most liberal members of the royal family—has welcomed Abdullah's reforms but argues that they are inadequate to move Saudi Arabia fully into the twenty-first century. "In order to survive," Talal told me, "the kingdom has to adapt itself to the new world and become fully integrated into the globalized economy." To do so, he believes, more fundamental reforms are needed. Saudi Arabia must join the World Trade Organization (WTO), for example; indeed, Riyadh has been trying to do just that for seven years but has been denied entry for its failure to make the required judicial, social, and political changes. This irks the prince. "As a patriot and a democrat," he declared, "I would like to see my country endowed with a transparent political system and with laws that are passed by a representative assembly, which would also approve the state budget." Among other items on the prince's wish list are equal rights for women, a totally independent judiciary, the removal of archaic laws from the books, the holding of municipal elections, a modernized educational system adapted to the needs of the country, the "humanization" of penal sanctions ("some of which were inherited from pre-Islamic times," according to the prince), a liberalization of social life (for example, allowing theaters and movie houses), and "state neutrality and tolerance toward all religions." "Nothing in my proposals is contrary to Islam," argues Talal. "Quite the contrary; the religious and political foundations of the kingdom would be consolidated through them."

The conservative wing of the royal family disagrees, however, maintaining that the reforms would destabilize the regime by provoking the opposition of both the religious establishment and a conservative population imbued with Wahhabi dogma. The reformists counter that there is nothing so revolutionary about the proposals; they point out that during the reign of Ibn Saud, the founder of the kingdom, churches were allowed to function, banks collected and paid interest, and women legally enjoyed more freedom than they do today. Reformers also point out that Ibn Saud and one of his successors, King Faisal, managed to impose unpopular reforms—sometimes through the use of force—including the suppression of slavery, the opening of schools for girls, and the introduction of television. And they did all this without undermining the regime. Moreover, although reformers recognize that the kingdom was built on an alliance between the Wahhabi clergy and the House of Saud, they note that the government was always meant to maintain the upper hand, in keeping with an Islamic tradition that recognizes the primacy of the temporal over the spiritual in state affairs.

In any alliance, however, it is the balance of power that determines which partner dominates. From the 1940s to the 1970s, the House of Saud held all the cards and thus overshadowed the clergy. Two factors have since helped change that situation. First, the royal family has lost influence due to the excesses of certain of its members, who have been accused of abusing their excessive privileges, of leading dissolute lives marked by corruption and wasteful spending, and of inordinate submissiveness to U.S. wishes. A second factor has been the emergence of a militant fringe of Islamists under the tutelage of the Muslim Brotherhood. These radicals, such as bin Laden, have called into question the very legitimacy of the al Saud dynasty, and although it is impossible to gauge the precise impact of such propaganda, it appears to have resonated. Meanwhile, the ongoing deterioration of economic and social conditions has reduced the clout of the ruling family still further.

When first faced with these challenges, the Saudi royals made an ill-conceived decision to come to terms with their adversaries rather than confront them. When an armed revolt by Islamic extremists broke out in 1979 in Mecca, the authorities dealt ruthlessly with the perpetrators but were strangely indulgent toward those who had inspired them. A similar situation followed the Gulf War of 1991. The war was opposed by a number of religious figures, some of whom were jailed, but those given long prison terms were eventually released early, and political concessions were made to the radical wing of the clergy. Religious education was intensified in the schools and universities, including in science departments; girls' schools were placed under the direct control of the religious authorities (although the ministry of education reportedly regained jurisdiction last spring); women were forbidden to sing on radio or television or in public; and increased powers were granted to the *mutawaun* (volunteers), a clerical police force whose task is to "promote virtue" by making sure that public establishments close during the hours of prayer (five times a day) and by taking into custody women and young people whose conduct is not in keeping with "Islamic morals." The clergy was also given effective censorship power over the media, especially radio and television.

These concessions, according to numerous reformists, were as unnecessary as they were dangerous. They were made to a vocal minority that should have been suppressed rather than placated. Reformists argue that the great majority of the religious establishment—officials whose salaries are paid by the state—would have remained loyal to the royal family without the compromises. The fidelity of this silent majority of clergy has long been virtually guaranteed by the many privileges they enjoy, privileges that enable them to enrich themselves through speculative ventures—for example, by selling at high prices land received as a gift from the state. Afforded the same diplomatic immunity as members of the royal family, clerics cannot be arrested or put on trial without the explicit authorization of the palace. Small wonder, then, that most remain loyal to their benefactors. Indeed, this loyalty was recently demonstrated by their quiet acquiescence to Prince Abdullah's peace plan.

And yet the state has consistently bowed to militants and conservatives, and liberals—religious and otherwise—have been condemned to silence. The authorities even intervened in August 2001 to censor a Web site that the reformists had established in London with secret financing by certain members of the royal family. Moreover, conservative clerics have been allowed to dominate the media. As a result, there has been no national debate on the gradual transformation of the kingdom, and reformers have found few outlets to garner support.

Contrary to the contention of the conservatives, however, most Saudis would be amenable to the modernization of their state—if it could be carried out without violating the fundamental principles of Islam, as has been achieved in some moderate Muslim countries. Especially supportive of such reforms are Saudi women, young people, business leaders, technocrats, and the enlightened intelligentsia—not to mention the liberal wing of the royal family. Together, these forces make up more than half of the population. They believe that change need not be destabilizing; according to one young prince with an important government position, "democratization would have the advantage of increasing the legitimacy of the ruling family. Unfortunately," he continued, "we are ruled by a gerontocracy that prefers the artificial comfort of the status quo."

As for which side will prevail, Enazy, for his part, is pessimistic. He believes that the Wahhabi kingdom is going through "a Brezhnevian period. But no one here wants to play the role of [Mikhail] Gorbachev, who ushered in the collapse of the communist system." Rather than Russia, however, the more apposite analogy may be with Iran. Crown Prince Abdullah, like Iranian President Muhammad Khatami, has become the standard-bearer for a reformist majority that lacks the means to realize its aspirations. Both leaders are prisoners of a political and religious system dominated by a conservative faction that, although perhaps not representative of the populace, nonetheless controls the levers of power. Prince Abdullah cannot act without a consensus within the royal family, which is dominated by a powerful group of his half brothers known as the "Sudeiri Seven." This group includes the king and his six full brothers (whose mother belongs to the Sudeiri family); they control key positions in the realm, including the defense ministry, the interior ministry, the treasury, and the governorships of the main provinces. Although the royal family is far from monolithic, none of its more liberal members is prepared to confront this powerful bloc; after all, dissension within the House of Saud could unleash dangerous chaos.

Having said that, the reformists have failed to capitalize on what strengths they do possess. Unorganized and amorphous, they represent various schools of thought and segments of society, from business leaders calling for transparency in state affairs to democrats advocating universal suffrage, from constitutional monarchists and Wahhabi modernists to determined secularists.

Given this lack of cohesion, even liberal members of the royal family fear that, if given free rein, the reformists, lacking any one clear agenda, could get out of hand.

The fundamental truth, however, remains that radical change would spell the end of the al Saud family's absolute power and the privileges enjoyed by some 3,000 princes and the hundreds of families linked to them. This is the real source of the government's conservatism, and helps explain why Prince Abdullah, like President Khatami—both of whom have a stake in the survival of the system—has proceeded so cautiously. There is no doubt that the crown prince fully intends to carry on with his efforts to modernize the state and to promote economic development. But the extent and the pace of his reforms will depend less on his intentions than on the internal tensions of a society riddled with contradictions, and on the external pressures engendered by the irresistible push toward globalization. ☯

Next Stop Baghdad?

Kenneth M. Pollack

CUTTING THE GORDIAN KNOT

As THE CONFLICT in Afghanistan winds down, the question of what the United States should do about Iraq has risen to the forefront of American foreign policy. Hawks argue that toppling Saddam Hussein should be "phase two" in the war on terrorism. They see Iraq's development of unconventional weapons as a critical threat to U.S. national interests and want to parlay the success of the Afghan campaign into a similar operation further west. Those who pass for doves in the mainstream debate point to the difficulty of such an undertaking and the lack of any evidence tying Saddam to the recent attacks on the United States. They argue that the goal of America's Iraq policy should be to revive U.N. weapons inspections and re-energize containment. Both camps have it partly right—and partly wrong.

Thanks to Washington's own missed opportunities and others' shameful cynicism, there are no longer any good policy options toward Iraq. The hawks are wrong to think the problem is desperately urgent or connected to terrorism, but they are right to see the prospect of a nuclear-armed Saddam as so worrisome that it requires drastic action. The doves, meanwhile, are right about Iraq's not being a good candidate for a replay of Operation Enduring Freedom, but they are wrong to think that inspections and deterrence are adequate responses to Iraq's weapons of mass destruction (WMD) programs.

KENNETH M. POLLACK is Senior Fellow and Deputy Director for National Security Studies at the Council on Foreign Relations. From 1999 to 2001 he served as Director for Gulf Affairs on the staff of the National Security Council.

Next Stop Baghdad?

After the more immediate danger posed by Osama bin Laden's al Qaeda network has been dealt with, the Bush administration should indeed turn its attention to Baghdad. What it should do at that point, however, is pursue the one strategy that offers a way out of the impasse. The United States should invade Iraq, eliminate the present regime, and pave the way for a successor prepared to abide by its international commitments and live in peace with its neighbors.

THE TROUBLE WITH CONTAINMENT

THE REASONS for contemplating such dramatic action have little to do with the events of September 11 and the subsequent crisis and much to do with the course of U.S. policy toward Iraq since 1991. After Iraq's defeat in the Persian Gulf War, the first Bush administration hoped Saddam would fall from power. It had no clear strategy for how to make that happen, however, and so settled for keeping him isolated and defanged until the lucky day eventually arrived. For lack of a better alternative the Clinton administration continued the same policy, as has the current administration.

The central goal of containment over the past decade has been to prevent Saddam—a serial aggressor—from rebuilding Iraq's military power, including its weapons of mass destruction. The United States and its allies did not want to have to deter, repel, or reverse another Iraqi invasion; they wanted to deny Saddam the wherewithal to mount a threat to his neighbors in the first place. So they put in place, under U.N. auspices, a combination of economic, military, and diplomatic constraints that prevented Saddam from once again destabilizing one of the world's most strategically important regions, while simultaneously allowing humanitarian exemptions so Iraq could meet the nonmilitary needs of its population. Despite the criticism it often received, this policy was a sensible approach to a situation in which there were few attractive options. It served its purposes well, and far longer than most thought possible.

Over the last few years, however, containment has started to unravel. Serious inspections of Saddam's WMD programs stopped long ago. Fewer and fewer nations respect the U.N.-mandated constraints, and more and more are tired of constantly battling with Saddam to force him to comply. Ludicrous Iraqi propaganda about how the economic sanctions are responsible for the deaths of more than a million people since 1991 is now accepted at face value the world over. A dozen or more nations have flown commercial airliners into Iraq to flout the ban on air travel to and from the country—a ban they now claim never existed, but one that was a well-respected fact just a few years ago. Smuggled Iraqi oil flows via Jordan, Syria, Turkey, and the Persian Gulf states at a rate more than double what it was in 1998. Iraq is increasingly able to get its hands on prohibited items such as spare parts for its tanks and planes and equipment for its crippled logistical system. Most stunning of all, the Chinese were recently caught building a nation-wide fiber-optic communications network for Saddam's regime; the key nodes of this system were destroyed by U.S. airstrikes in January 2001. If respect for the sanctions has already eroded to the point where the Chinese are willing to sell Iraq such critical technology, how long will it be before someone proves willing to sell tanks? Or missiles? Or fissile material?

Repeated calls to resuscitate the anti-Saddam coalition and strengthen containment are correct about the problem but naïve in thinking it can be solved easily. Comprehensive sanctions of the type imposed on Iraq are of necessity a multilateral effort, and at this point there are simply too many important countries willing to subvert them for the scheme to be effective. The current administration's unhappy experience in trying to sell "smart sanctions" to the international community shows just how bad the situation is. The administration's proposed reforms would lift most of the economic constraints on Iraq in return for tighter controls over what comes into the country—a perfectly reasonable idea for anyone actually interested in helping the Iraqi people while keeping Saddam's military in check. But France, Russia, China, and others have opposed the plan because Baghdad fears, correctly, that if it were accepted some form of international military and financial controls might be prolonged.

Ironically, in practice the smart sanctions probably would not do much more than briefly stave off containment's collapse. Right now the U.N. uses its control over Iraq's contracts to determine what goes into and out of the country legally. The system is policed through U.N. (read U.S.) scrutiny of every Iraqi contract—a cumbersome and glacially slow process that still fails to stop Saddam's massive smuggling activities. The Bush administration's proposal would shift the enforcement burden away from the U.N. and onto Iraq's neighbors and try to shut down illegal trade by buying the cooperation of those states through which it would have to pass— Jordan, Syria, Turkey, Iran, and the members of the Gulf Cooperation Council (Bahrain, Kuwait, Oman, Qatar, Saudi Arabia, and the United Arab Emirates). The problem is that all these countries profit from the smuggling, all have populations opposed to enforcing the sanctions, and all except the GCC and Iran are now highly vulnerable to Iraqi economic pressure. So no matter what they may say publicly, none of them is likely to help much in blocking the flow of oil, money, and contraband.

At this point, restoring a serious and sustainable containment regime would require an entirely new set of arrangements. General economic sanctions would have to be lifted and the current U.N. contracting system virtually eliminated, while the core military embargo and financial controls would have to be left in place, harsh penalties instituted for violators, and preauthorization arranged for the use of force by the United States to compel compliance. Such a deal is unimaginable in the U.N. Security Council today, where many of the members compete to see who can appease Iraq most. And although in theory similar reforms could be imposed by the United States unilaterally, any attempt to do so would soon run into passionate international opposition, crippling U.S. diplomacy long before it had much effect on Saddam. Reforming containment enough to make it viable, therefore, is simply not in the offing.

THE TROUBLE WITH DETERRENCE

IN RESPONSE to the problems of containment, some have argued that the United States should fall back on a strategy of deterrence—or rather, containment as it was actually practiced against the Soviet Union during the Cold War (as opposed to the super-sized version applied to Iraq in the 1990s). This would mean allowing the post–Gulf War constraints to slip away altogether and relying solely on the threat of U.S. intervention to dissuade Saddam from future aggression. Such an approach would be generally welcome outside the United States. But it would involve running a terrible risk, for it is not at all clear that Saddam can be deterred successfully for very long.

This is not to argue that Saddam is irrational. There is considerable evidence that he weighs costs and benefits, follows a crude logic in determining how best to achieve his goals, understands deterrence, and has been deterred in the past. Few knowledgeable observers doubt that Saddam refrained from using WMD when he attacked Israel during the Gulf War because he feared Israeli nuclear retaliation, and he seems to have been deterred from using WMD against Saudi Arabia and coalition forces because he feared U.S. retaliation.

Nevertheless, Saddam has a number of pathologies that make deterring him unusually difficult. He is an inveterate gambler and risk-taker who regularly twists his calculation of the odds to suit his preferred course of action. He bases his calculations on assumptions that outsiders often find bizarre and has little understanding of the larger world. He is a solitary decision-maker who relies little on advice from others. And he has poor sources of information about matters outside Iraq, along with intelligence services that generally tell him what they believe he wants to hear. These pathologies lie behind the many terrible miscalculations Saddam has made over the years that flew in the face of deterrence—including the invasion of Iran in 1980, the invasion of Kuwait in 1990, the decision to fight for Kuwait in 1990–91, and the decision to threaten Kuwait again in 1994.

It is thus impossible to predict the kind of calculations he would make about the willingness of the United States to challenge him once he had the ability to incinerate Riyadh, Tel Aviv, or the Saudi oil fields. He might well make another grab for Kuwait, for example, and once in possession dare the United States to evict him and risk a nuclear exchange. During the Cold War, U.S. strategists used to fret that once the Soviet Union reached strategic parity, Moscow would feel free to employ its conventional forces as it saw fit because the United States would be too scared of escalation to respond. Such fears were plausible in the abstract but seem to have been groundless because Soviet leaders were fundamentally conservative decision-makers. Saddam, in contrast, is fundamentally aggressive and risk-acceptant. Leaving him free to acquire nuclear weapons and then hoping that in spite of his track record he can be deterred this time around is not the kind of social science experiment the United States government should be willing to run.

PHASE TWO?

WITH CONTAINMENT eroding and deterrence too risky, some form of regime change is steadily becoming the only answer to the Iraqi conundrum. In the wake of the September 11 attacks, in fact, supporters of one particular approach to regime change—using the Iraqi opposition to do the job, in conjunction with U.S. air power—have repackaged their ideas to fit the times and gained substantial momentum. The position of these hawks was captured succinctly in a September 20 "open letter" to President Bush from three dozen luminaries, who argued that

> any strategy aiming at the eradication of terrorism and its sponsors must include a determined effort to remove Saddam Hussein from power in Iraq. Failure to undertake such an effort will constitute an early and perhaps decisive surrender in the war on international terrorism. The United States must therefore provide full military and financial support to the Iraqi opposition. American military force should be used to provide a "safe zone" in Iraq from which the opposition can operate.

Once the military operations in Afghanistan succeeded, they were widely touted by such hawks as a model for a future campaign against Saddam.

The hawks are right on two big points: that a nuclear-armed Saddam would be a disaster waiting to happen and that at this point it would be easier to get rid of him than to stop him from reconstituting his weapons programs. Unfortunately, most of them are wrong on key details, such as how regime change should be accomplished. Trying to topple Saddam by using the same limited military approach the United States used in Afghanistan—air power, special forces, and support for local opposition groups—would be trying to do the job on the cheap, and like all such efforts would run a real risk of disaster. It is possible that the Afghan strategy would work against Iraq—but not likely.

In recent wars, U.S. air power has repeatedly proven devastating, and against Iraq it could by itself undoubtedly accomplish numerous missions. A determined air campaign that focused on Saddam's key supporters—the Republican Guard, the Special Republican Guard, the Baath Party, the Saddam Fedayeen, and the internal security services—might spark a coup. Indeed, in December 1998 Operation Desert Fox struck at this target set and Saddam became so concerned about a coup that he overreacted, ordering emergency security measures, including the arrest and assassination of several important Shi`ite clerics, that set off uprisings among Iraq's Shi`a communities. If the intention is to coerce Saddam into respecting U.N. sanctions or modest U.S. dictates, then an open-ended air campaign along the lines of Desert Fox would likely do the trick.

But coercing Saddam by threatening his overthrow is one thing, and making sure that overthrow occurs is another. The fact is that Desert Fox did not produce a coup, and the unrest that Saddam created through his overreaction was easily suppressed. All available evidence indicates that even an Afghan-style war effort would have little chance of eliminating the regime in Iraq, because of the many differences between the two cases.

In Afghanistan, the military balance between the opposition and the Taliban was quite close, which is why limited U.S. actions were able to tip the scales decisively. The Northern Alliance fighters had frustrated the much larger and better-armed Taliban forces on the battlefield for seven years. Although the Taliban slowly gained control over most of the country, the Northern Alliance always gave ground grudgingly, making the Taliban pay for every step. In Iraq, in contrast, the gap in capabilities between the regime and the opposition is much wider. In 1991 and again in 1996, Saddam's

Republican Guard easily defeated even the strongest of the local Iraqi opposition forces, the two Kurdish militias. If the United States were to provide the Kurds with weapons, training, funds, and massive air support, at some point they would probably be able to hold their territory against an Iraqi assault—but even then they would have great difficulty translating such a defensive capability into the offensive power needed to overthrow Saddam.

Some argue that with U.S. aid the external Iraqi opposition, principally the Iraq National Congress (INC), could play the Northern Alliance role. But the INC has several big strikes against it. None of Iraq's neighbors is willing to serve as a sanctuary for it because they consider it ineffectual. The INC lacks competent field commanders and has never demonstrated any serious support inside Iraq. Even with U.S. help and a base of operations in northern Iraq from 1992 to 1996, it could never gather more than a few hundred fighters at a time, was heavily reliant on the Kurds for military operations, and was unable to secure any significant defections from the Iraqi armed forces.

If the Iraqi opposition is much weaker than the Northern Alliance, the Iraqi regime is also much stronger than the Taliban was. The Taliban fielded perhaps 45,000 troops, while Iraq has armed forces totaling 400,000—one-quarter of them in the elite Republican Guard and Special Republican Guard—along with paramilitary forces totaling hundreds of thousands more. The Iraqi army is much better armed than the Taliban was, has better discipline, and has demonstrated better unit cohesion. The Iraqi armed forces are hardly a juggernaut, but they have repeatedly proved to be more than a match for all local opposition.

Saddam's control over Iraq, meanwhile, is much stronger than the Taliban's control was over Afghanistan. He has quashed countless coup attempts, insurrections, and even outright revolts during his decades in power, and this has made the average Iraqi very wary of taking action of any kind against his regime. It is true that following Saddam's catastrophic defeat in the Gulf War there were major rebellions throughout southern Iraq. But what is noteworthy about them is not how large they were, but how small. Despite the magnitude of Saddam's defeat, only several tens of thousands of people ever joined in the uprisings. Despite their passionate hatred of Saddam, the vast majority of Iraqis were so terrified of him that they chose to wait to see how things would turn out rather than join the rebellion and risk retribution if it failed.

WOULD THIS TIME BE DIFFERENT?

THE KEY to victory in Afghanistan was a U.S. air campaign that routed the Taliban combat forces, leaving the Northern Alliance only the tasks of reducing several isolated strongholds and generally mopping up. In Iraq, U.S. air power would have to accomplish at least the same results for an Afghan-style strategy to succeed, but on this score history is not encouraging.

In Operation Desert Storm, the United States hit Iraq with what was probably the most powerful preliminary air campaign in history. It followed this up with one of the most decisive ground campaigns of the twentieth century. By early March 1991, the Iraqi armed forces had been reduced to a shadow of their former selves. Yet weak as they were, they still had enough strength to crush the largest insurrections in Iraqi history and keep Saddam in power. Those who favor the Afghan approach against Iraq are therefore betting that a U.S. military effort significantly smaller than the one mounted in 1991 would somehow produce much greater results this time around.

Some claim that U.S. and Iraqi forces today are so different from those a decade ago that such history is no longer relevant. Iraq's military is certainly not as capable as it once was. And since 1991, improvements in command, control, communications, and intelligence capabilities, together with the greater availability and effectiveness of precision-guided munitions, have made the U.S. military machine far more deadly. In one crucial area, however—the ability to break enemy ground forces using air strikes alone—the vast strides the U.S. military has taken since 1991 have yielded only a modest improvement.

Most of the U.S. advances have come in using fewer forces to destroy a given target. But throughout history the key determinant of whether ground units are likely to collapse from air strikes alone has not been the accuracy of the blows, but rather the commitment and discipline of the troops being struck. This point was reinforced in Afghanistan, where the less committed Taliban troops broke under U.S. airstrikes but the more determined and disciplined al Qaeda units did not—and fought hard later at Kunduz, Kandahar, and Tora Bora.

The same was true during the Gulf War, when Iraq's low-grade infantry divisions broke under the massive U.S. air campaign, but the more determined and disciplined Republican Guard and regular army heavy divisions did not. This was hardly for lack of trying. The coalition flew 110,000 sorties against Iraq during Desert Storm, compared to only 6,500 against the Taliban by the fall of Kandahar. It hit the key Republican Guard divisions with more than 1,000 sorties apiece, used twice as many precision-guided munitions against Iraq as against the Taliban, and destroyed perhaps 1,500 Iraqi armored fighting vehicles from the air. The United States waged a far more punishing air campaign against Iraq than it did against the Taliban, in other words, and inflicted far more damage on Iraqi forces. But the key Iraqi divisions never broke and fought hard, although not particularly well, during the coalition's subsequent ground offensive. The odds are, therefore, that even today a substantial part of Saddam's forces would weather a sustained aerial attack, and even badly battered would still be able to prevail in combat against the opposition afterward.

Using the Afghan approach in Iraq, moreover, would leave the United States dangerously vulnerable to Saddam's counterattacks. Once Saddam realized that Washington was serious about regime change, he would fight back with everything he had—including the two or three dozen Scud-type missiles with biological and chemical warheads that U.N. inspectors and U.S. intelligence believe he has stashed away. During the Gulf War, the United States was unable to find Iraq's Scud launchers in the western and southern parts of the country even though it used large numbers of aircraft and special forces teams in the effort. American capabilities have improved since then, but few in the U.S. military have confidence that the same mix of forces would do much better today. Likewise, once an Afghan-style air campaign began, Saddam would have every incentive to crush the Kurds. Since America's ability to defend them without ground forces is extremely limited, it has relied on deterrence—the threat of a massive air campaign—instead. If such an air campaign is going on anyway, that threat will no longer work, and Saddam would likely move to reoccupy the north—with all of the attendant slaughter and repression that would entail.

Saddam might also decide to shut down Iraqi oil production to try to force Washington to halt its attacks. The U.S. strategic petroleum reserve could compensate for the loss of Iraqi oil for about seven months, but the uncertain length of an Afghan-style campaign against Iraq would raise the possibility that U.S. reserves might run out before Saddam fell. Unless U.S. ground forces occupied the Iraqi oil fields at the start of a war, moreover, there would be little to prevent Saddam from destroying them as a final act of vengeance, just as he destroyed Kuwait's oil fields in 1991.

Carrying off an Afghan-style campaign against Iraq, finally, would be extremely difficult without the support of a number of regional partners—to provide bases and overflight for the air campaign, conduits and safe havens for the opposition forces, help with making up any shortfalls in Iraqi oil production, and so forth. Indeed, the Afghan operations themselves required help from countries including Pakistan, Uzbekistan, Kyrgyzstan, Tajikistan, Russia, and India. A replay against Iraq, a much larger and harder target, would require a comparable lineup of local friends.

Unfortunately, this is the one approach to the problem that the frontline states have made clear they would not support. America's allies in the region have told Washington time and again that they will not assist any U.S. military operation with an indeterminate end and low chances of success. As one high-ranking GCC official has put it, "when you are ready to use all of your forces we will be there for you, but we're not interested in letting you try out theories about air power."

THE CASE FOR INVASION

SADDAM HUSSEIN must be dealt with. But thinking about Iraq in the context of the war on terrorism or the operations in Afghanistan obscures more than it clarifies. Given the specific features of the Iraqi situation, trying to topple Saddam with an Afghan-style campaign would be risky and ill advised. It might just work, but there is no reason to chance it, especially since adding a major ground component—that is, replaying the Gulf War rather than the Afghan campaign—would not cost much more while making success a near certainty. Even without committing its own ground forces, the United States would still be responsible for Iraq's political and military reconstruction. Using a standoff approach to regime change, however, would limit American ability to control events while opening the door to mischief-makers who would try to turn Saddam's fall to their own advantage. Because of the human, diplomatic, and financial costs involved, invasion should always be a last resort. Unfortunately in this case, since all the other options are worse, it is a necessary one.

The strategic logic for invasion is compelling. It would eliminate the possibility that Saddam might rebuild his military or acquire nuclear weapons and thus threaten the security of the world's supply of oil. It would allow the United States to redeploy most of its forces away from the region afterward, or at the very least return to its pre–Gulf War "over the horizon" presence—something long sought by locals and the United States alike. And by facilitating the recon-struction of Iraq and its re-entry into regional politics it would remove a major irritant from U.S. relations with the Muslim world in general.

The military aspects of an invasion, meanwhile, although hardly painless, would be straightforward and well within U.S. capabilities. In 1991, U.S. forces ran roughshod over their Iraqi counterparts, and in the ten years since then the gap in capabilities between the two sides has widened. At this point, the United States could probably smash Iraq's ground forces with a single corps composed of two heavy divisions and an armored cavalry regiment. To be on the safe side and to handle other missions, however, it would make sense to plan for a force twice that size. Some light infantry will be required in case Saddam's loyalists fight in Iraq's cities. Airmobile forces will be needed to seize Iraq's oil fields at the start of hostilities and to occupy the sites from which Saddam could launch missiles against Israel or Saudi Arabia. And troops will have to be available for occupation duties once the fighting is over. All told, the force should total roughly

200,000–300,000 people: for the invasion, between four and six divisions plus supporting units, and for the air campaign, 700–1,000 aircraft and anywhere from one to five carrier battle groups (depending on what sort of access to bases turned out to be possible). Building up such a force in the Persian Gulf would take three to five months, but the campaign itself would probably take about a month, including the opening air operations.

The casualties incurred during such an operation might well be greater than during the Afghan or Gulf Wars, but they are unlikely to be catastrophic. Two factors that could increase the toll would be the willingness of Iraqi forces to fight tenaciously for their cities and a decision by Saddam to employ unconventional weapons during the crisis. On the other hand, it is possible that the mere presence of such American forces on Iraq's doorstep could produce a coup that would topple Saddam without significant combat.

The military aspects of an invasion, actually, are likely to be the easiest part of the deal. The diplomatic fallout will probably be more difficult, with its severity directly related to the length of the campaign and the certainty of its outcome. Just as in Afghanistan, the longer it drags on and the more uncertain it looks, the more dissent will be heard, both at home and abroad—whereas the quicker and more decisive the victory, the more palatable it will be for all concerned.

The only country whose support would be absolutely necessary for an invasion is Kuwait. The task would be made dramatically easier if the Saudis helped, however, both because of the excellent bases on their territory and because the GCC and Jordan would undoubtedly follow the Saudi lead. Although both the Saudis and the Kuwaitis have said they do not want the United States to attack Iraq, the consensus among those who know those countries' leaders well is that they would grudgingly consent if the United States could convince them it was willing to use the full range of its military capabilities to ensure a swift, successful campaign.

Egyptian permission would be required to move ships through the Suez Canal and planes across its airspace, but given the importance of U.S. economic and military assistance to Egypt that should not be a problem. Turkey's support would also be useful, in particular because it would make it much easier to defend the

Kurds in northern Iraq from an Iraqi counteroffensive. Other regional states would have an incentive to come on board because they would want to have a say in the postinvasion political arrangements in Baghdad. The French, the Russians, and the Chinese would object strongly to the whole concept and might try to kill it by raising a diplomatic firestorm. Still, they could not stop a U.S. invasion were the administration truly set on one, and they might eventually jump on board once it went ahead if only to retain political and economic influence in Iraq later on.

The biggest headaches for the United States are likely to stem not from the invasion itself but from its aftermath. Once the country has been conquered and Saddam's regime driven from power, the United States would be left "owning" a country of 22 million people ravaged by more than two decades of war, totalitarian misrule, and severe deprivation. The invaders would get to decide the composition and form of a future Iraqi government—both an opportunity and a burden. Some form of unitary but federalized state would probably best suit the bewildering array of local and foreign interests involved, but ideally this decision would be a collective one: as in Afghanistan, the United States should try to turn the question of future Iraqi political arrangements over to the U.N., or possibly the Arab League, thus shedding and spreading some responsibility for the outcome. Alternatively, it might bring in those countries most directly affected by the outcome—the Saudis, Kuwaitis, Jordanians, and Turks—both to co-opt them and as an incentive for their diplomatic support. In the end, of course, it would be up to the United States to make sure that a post-Saddam Iraq did not slip into chaos like Lebanon in the 1980s or Afghanistan in the 1990s, creating spillover effects in the region and raising the possibility of a new terrorist haven.

Because it will be important to ensure that Iraq does not fall apart afterward, the United States will also need to repair much of the damage done to the Iraqi economy since Saddam's accession. It could undoubtedly raise substantial funds for this purpose from the GCC and perhaps some European and East Asian allies dependent on Persian Gulf oil. And as soon as Iraq's oil started flowing again, the country could contribute to its own future. Current estimates of the cost of rebuilding Iraq's economy, however, range from $50 billion to $150 billion, and that does not include repairing the damage from yet another major war. The United States should thus be prepared to contribute several billion dollars per year for as much as a decade to rebuild the country.

IF NOT NOW, WHEN?

IT IS ONE THING to recognize that because of the unique features of this case—the scale of the interests involved, Saddam's unparalleled record of aggression and violence, and the problems with other options—an invasion of Iraq is the least bad course of action available. It is another to figure out just when such an invasion should be launched. Despite what many hawks now argue, it is a mistake to think of operations against Iraq as part of the war on terrorism. The dilemma the United States must now grapple with, in fact, is that attacking Iraq could jeopardize the success of that war, but the longer it waits before attacking the harder it will be and the greater the risk that Saddam's strength will increase.

Toppling Saddam is not a necessary component of the war on terrorism, and by itself Iraq's support for terrorism would not justify the heavy costs of an invasion. Iraq is indeed a state sponsor of terrorism, but on the grand roll of such sponsors it is well behind Iran, Syria, Pakistan, Sudan, Lebanon, North Korea, Libya, and several others. If the only problem the United States had with Iraq were its support for terrorism, it would be a relatively minor concern. Conversely, if one were to list Saddam Hussein's crimes against humanity in order of their importance, his support for terrorism would rank low.

The reason for even contemplating all the costs that an invasion would entail is the risk that a nuclear-armed Saddam might wreak havoc in his region and beyond, together with the certainty that he will acquire such weapons eventually if left unchecked. Nevertheless, there is no indication that he is about to get them within weeks or months. Containment may be dying, but it is not dead yet, and a determined U.S. effort could keep it alive for some time longer. Iraq represents an emerging threat, but bin Laden and his accomplices constitute an immediate one.

Next Stop Baghdad?

Al Qaeda has demonstrated both the ability and the willingness to reach into the American homeland and slaughter thousands, and it now has the motive of revenge to add to its general ideological hostility. Breaking the network's back in Afghanistan and elsewhere should therefore be the Bush administration's top national security priority, and this cannot be done without the active cooperation of scores of U.S. allies around the world—for intelligence gathering, police work, and financial cooperation, all on top of any military or diplomatic help that might be required.

So far the administration's efforts in this area are paying off, largely because others have supported them. Should that trend continue, it is likely that within anywhere from six months to two years the United States and its partners will have disrupted al Qaeda's communications, recruitment, financing, and planning so much that what is left of the network will be largely innocuous. Until this point has been reached, it would be a mistake to jeopardize success by risking a major break with U.S. allies—something that a serious campaign against Iraq might well make necessary. And besides, laying the appropriate military, political, diplomatic, and economic groundwork for an invasion will take considerable time and effort.

Nevertheless, those calling for an immediate attack on Iraq make a legitimate point. Too much delay could be as problematic as too little, because it would risk the momentum gained from the victory over Afghanistan. Today the shock of the September 11 attacks is still fresh and the U.S. government and public are ready to make sacrifices—while the rest of the world recognizes American anger and may be leery of getting on the wrong side of it. The longer the wait before an invasion, the harder it will be to muster domestic and international support for it, even though the reason for invading would have little or nothing to do with Iraq's connection to terrorism. And over time the effort to take down al Qaeda could actually exacerbate the problems with containment, since some of America's partners in that effort want to loosen rather than tighten the noose on the Iraqi regime and may try to use the leverage of their cooperation with us to stall any bold moves. The United States can afford to wait a little while before turning to Saddam, in other words, but not indefinitely.

Even when a policy cannot be sustained forever, it often makes sense to spin out its final stages for as long as possible. This is not the case with the containment of Iraq today. The last two years have witnessed a dramatic erosion of the constraints on the Iraqi regime. The Bush administration's initial solution to this problem, the smart sanctions plan, would be little more than a Band-Aid and even so could not find general acceptance. If no more serious action is taken, the United States and the world at large may soon confront a nuclear-armed Saddam. At that point the danger would be obvious to all, but it would be infinitely more difficult to confront. Taking down al Qaeda should indeed be the priority of the moment, and using half-measures, such as the Afghan approach, against Saddam would be a mistake. But these should not become permanent excuses for inaction. We may tarry, but Saddam will not.☯

Iran in the Balance

Puneet Talwar

BACKLASH

SOON AFTER reformists won a landslide victory in Iran's February 2000 parliamentary elections, the conservative offensive began in earnest. One of the first victims was Saeed Hajjarian, a top strategist in the reform movement and among President Mohammad Khatami's closest advisers, who was on his way to a meeting of Tehran's city council when a young man hopped off a motorcycle and approached him. The man pulled a gun, pointed it at Hajjarian's head, and fired. The reformist survived the attack, although he was critically wounded, and the gunman and several accomplices were eventually tried and imprisoned. Still, few Iranians believe the attackers acted on their own, and the incident drove home the extraordinary risks now facing Iran's reformers. The shooting also marked the beginning of a sustained assault on the reform movement that has continued ever since.

Anxious to turn back Khatami's democratic reforms, hard-line conservatives are now resorting to ever more aggressive tactics. On March 4 of this year, Mostafa Tajzadeh—Iran's deputy interior minister and another Khatami confidant—was sentenced to a year in prison by the conservative judiciary. The trumped-up conviction, ostensibly for rigging votes in last year's parliamentary victory by the reformists, was an attempt by hard-liners to prevent Tajzadeh from overseeing the June 8 presidential election.

PUNEET TALWAR served on the State Department's Policy Planning Staff from 1999 to 2001 and recently joined the staff of the Senate Foreign Relations Committee. He prepared this article while on a Council on Foreign Relations International Affairs Fellowship; the views expressed here are his own.

Tajzadeh was not the only recent victim. Reformist parliamentarians have been harassed and intimidated, and numerous media outlets have been shut down. The vehemence of the conservative backlash may stem from the hard-liners' fear that they are soon to be eclipsed. Despite all the attempts to stymie the reform movement, the Iranian public has endorsed further change at almost every opportunity—and, as of this writing, was expected to do so again by electing President Khatami to a second term with a wide margin on June 8. Still, the fate of Iran's democratic movement remains very much uncertain. Despite the popularity of the reformists, conservatives still dominate much of the government. The circumstances are so fragile that relatively minor changes could have dramatic repercussions inside Iran, eventually tilting the balance one way or another. American policy toward Iran should therefore proceed very carefully. Although it is clear what outcome Washington would prefer, the United States should avoid embracing any particular domestic faction as Iran's power struggle intensifies.

This does not mean, however, that Washington should do nothing at all. The right American policy—one characterized by subtle but significant shifts—could make an important contribution, encouraging Iran's evolution in a direction that would eventually benefit both countries. It is therefore time for the Bush administration to abandon the containment strategy it inherited and embark on a new policy of moderate engagement. By slowly helping Tehran reintegrate into the world community through various multilateral arrangements, Washington can encourage and strengthen positive forces within Iran. This tactic could eventually lead to a rapprochement between the two long-time enemies.

Given the legacy of mistrust between Tehran and Washington and the fluid nature of Iranian politics, rebuilding ties will take time. But Washington should start making the investment now, for Iran's strategic value is difficult to overlook. The country abuts the fragile states of the Caucasus and Central Asia, some of which are endowed with large untapped energy reserves. Iran's neighborhood also features oil-rich U.S. allies, a recalcitrant Iraq, a terrorist and narcotics haven known as Afghanistan, and a politically troubled, nuclear-armed Pakistan.

Most important, Iran's potential for democratic development far outstrips that of many of its troubled neighbors. If encouraged, the country could become a stabilizing force in a region vital to American interests. Improved U.S.-Iranian ties could lead to cooperation on a range of shared priorities. From the Iranian perspective, cooperation would lead to even greater prizes: the economic benefits that would accrue from normal commercial relations with the United States and the diplomatic gains that would accompany an end to Washington's containment policy.

That policy is already beginning to waver. In March 2000, the Clinton administration responded to reforms in Iran by making an explicit overture to

PRESIDENT MOHAMMAD KHATAMI

the Iranian people and their government. But the olive branch was rebuffed, and Tehran has continued to engage in the sort of activity that makes rapprochement impossible. Its tradition of supporting terrorism has not diminished: when violence between Israelis and Palestinians escalated last year, Iran gave both moral and material support to terrorist groups such as Hezbollah and Hamas, encouraging them to join forces in the fight against Israel. Meanwhile, within Iran, the government has continued to commit human rights violations and to develop missiles and weapons of mass destruction (WMD) with the assistance of Russia and other states. These are not minor obstacles to better relations with the United States, and because of them, crafting the right strategy for the Bush administration will not be easy. But Iran is slowly changing, and although the advances remain uncertain, it is time that U.S. policy followed suit.

LIBERATION THEOLOGIST

THE CURRENT dramatic changes in Iran date back to 1997 and the surprise election of a dark horse presidential candidate, a mid-level cleric named Mohammed Khatami, who came to power promising to democratize the Islamic Republic. Initially, Khatami succeeded in advancing large portions of his reform program (dubbed the "Second of *Khordad* Movement," after the date of his election on the Iranian calendar). Khatami and his allies granted new freedoms to the press, eased some social restrictions, and brought a limited degree of accountability to government. Iranians allowed themselves to become optimistic about the future.

Changes soon began to appear on the international front as well. In a 1998 interview on CNN, Khatami told a surprised world audience that he wanted to start breaking down "the wall of mistrust" that separated Iran from the United States. This statement was cautiously welcomed by much of the international community, which hoped that the positive changes being made inside Iran would eventually be reflected in the country's external policies. Meanwhile, the United States found that international support for the American containment policy was beginning to slip. As long as Iran had remained in the grip of revolutionary fervor, its extreme behavior helped justify U.S. policy. But once the new government reached out to the West, advocated détente with the United States, and called for democracy and the rule of law at home, international perceptions began to change. Key American allies in Europe had already embarked on a process of "critical dialogue" with Iran before Khatami's election, in the belief that engagement is a more effective way to reform a regime than is isolation. Once Khatami was inaugurated, Europe and Japan became even less willing to cooperate with the United States in applying pressure on Iran.

U.S. policymakers eventually began to moderate their views toward the Islamic Republic. In its final years, the Clinton administration started rethinking the aggressive containment policy that it had pursued since 1993—a policy that sought to isolate Iran, in part by attempting to limit all third-party assistance to the country. The restrictions had been tightened in 1995; in response to pressure from the Republican-dominated Congress, President Bill Clinton had issued an executive order imposing across-the-board, unilateral trade and investment sanctions on Iran. But in March 2000, Washington signaled its new approach toward Iran through a speech delivered by then Secretary of State Madeleine Albright. The speech touched on many painful historical episodes that still resonate strongly in both countries, such as American support for a 1953 coup and the 1979–81 hostage crisis. Albright then went on to outline a vision for a new, positive relationship between the United States and the Islamic Republic. She announced the easing of sanctions on Iranian exports of food and carpets and on people-to-people exchanges and offered to settle the significant legal claims that have remained unresolved for two decades since the revolution. And she reiterated the long-standing U.S. offer of open dialogue without any preconditions.

Albright's overture was received favorably by many in Iran who wanted improved ties with the United States. The speech even generated a brief, taboo-breaking debate on whether to restore relations with the United States—leading one Iranian newspaper to print an American flag, without any flames, on its front page. Unfortunately, the internal power struggle between reformists and conservatives soon intensified, leading most Iranians to turn their attention to matters closer to home. Tehran chose not to respond to the American offer.

THE HARD-LINERS STRIKE BACK

THE IMMEDIATE IMPETUS for Albright's speech had been the February 2000 election of a new parliament (or *Majlis*) dominated by the reformists. This victory marked the third time in three years in which Iranians had endorsed progressive change at the polls. After the election, many Iran-watchers believed that the reformists had finally gained the institutional clout they needed to begin implementing their program. But then the momentum changed rather abruptly.

In the last year, Khatami's moderates have been thrown on the defensive by a severe hard-line backlash, led by conservatives who still control Iran's courts, the Revolutionary Guards (an army-like institution that also plays an important role in internal security), the office of the Supreme Leader, and powerful bodies such as the Council of Guardians, which can veto legislation deemed to conflict with the Iranian constitution or Islamic principles. Under Iran's constitution, ultimate authority is vested in the Supreme Leader, who is appointed by a conservative-dominated council, establishes guidelines for Iran's domestic and foreign policies, and controls the state media, the judiciary, the Revolutionary Guards, the armed forces, and other key power centers. The president appoints a cabinet with the approval of parliament but occupies a secondary position, managing the day-to-day affairs of government within the parameters set by the Supreme Leader.

Using their institutional upper hand, hard-liners have arrested journalists and opposition political activists and sent them to prison. They have shut down reformist newspapers and magazines. Proposed laws debated by the *Majlis* to expand press freedom and promote social reforms have been blocked. The hard-liners have managed to harass and drive from office close associates of Khatami. The Second of *Khordad* Movement has stalled.

The battle lines, however, are not completely clear. Iran's political scene is vastly more complex than the simple division between "reformists" and "conservatives" suggests. In reality, each category encompasses a broad set of groups, each with its own ideology and world-view. The reformists include factions ranging from the religious left to pragmatic technocrats and restless students. The conservative label refers to diverse elements such as moderate *bazaaris* (merchants), much of the clerical establishment, and extreme hard-liners who advocate violence against their political opponents. To complicate matters even further, the two camps are not entirely consistent when it comes to Iran's foreign policy, including the question of relations with the United States. Elements in both camps take different positions on whether rapprochement is appropriate and on what conditions should be placed on a dialogue. Only one consistent factor distinguishes the two sides, in fact: the argument over the proper role and structure of government in Iran.

The two camps have also adopted different strategies. In recent months, the conservatives, especially the hard-line faction, have worked together effectively to weaken their opponents and slow or halt policies they view as threatening Iran's social harmony and the essence of the Islamic Republic. It remains unclear whether the conservatives have overreached and failed to recognize their own unpopularity with the public. For the time being, however, the reform movement has fallen into disarray—a reversal of roles from the first two and a half years of Khatami's tenure, when it was the conservatives who seemed on the defensive.

Many Iranians who had high hopes for the Second of *Khordad* Movement have been sorely disappointed, and some erstwhile supporters have directed their frustration at President Khatami for not assertively countering the challenges to his proposals. In recent months, Khatami has admitted candidly that he lacks the means to discharge his responsibilities. Despite his setbacks and the newly lowered expectations, however, Khatami was still (as of this writing) expected to win a second term easily. Though the scales may have fallen from the public's eyes, the president is still considered the best hope for peaceful reform.

A Khatami victory, however, will not by itself change the political dynamics in Iran. Despite a new popular mandate for the reformists, the conservatives—who have shown little interest in public sentiments thus far—will probably continue their assault on the president's reform agenda. But although the conservatives may succeed in slowing the pace of change, the underlying social and economic forces that led to Khatami's election in the first place will only continue to grow in strength. Iran today has a burgeoning youth culture: roughly half of the country's nearly 65 million people were born after the revolution. These young people crave social and political freedom and want their country to better integrate with the dynamic world beyond their borders. Along with a well-educated middle class, politically active women, and high unemployment, these forces form a potent combination that will ultimately make political change in Iran inevitable—whether the conservatives like it or not.

Khatami's program reflects these fundamental shifts in Iranian society. But the president, himself a cleric, has always taken extreme care to portray his reforms as consistent with the ideals of the revolution and Iran's constitutional order. Whether he will be able to carry it off and bridge the many competing forces within Iran while preserving his image as a champion of the Islamic Republic remains to be seen. Should Khatami fail, the broad coalition that carried him to power could split at the seams, with religious reformists, Western-oriented secularists, leftists, and students all going their separate ways.

THE MIDDLE PATH

GIVEN THIS UNCERTAINTY, the United States must avoid appearing to take sides in the ongoing power struggle. But this does not mean that Washington has no range of movement. In fact, the Bush administration has a choice of three broad options to follow in its Iran policy. One path would be either to simply continue with the Clinton approach (that is, basic containment but with some limited exceptions) or to try to reinvigorate it. A second option could be called "moderate engagement" and would involve helping Iran form better international ties while leaving key portions of the U.S. sanctions regime intact. This track could eventually lead Iran to moderate its more objectionable behavior and thus clear the way for improved U.S.-Iranian relations and the elimination of sanctions. A third option would be for Washington to take significant steps toward dismantling the sanctions regime now, with the hope that this preemptive move would jump-start a rapid rapprochement.

Maintaining the status quo might seem appealing to Bush officials, given the unpredictable and politically risky situation. But more of the same is unlikely to yield any progress with Iran in the foreseeable future. After eight years, there is no evidence that the current approach will ever convince Iran to modify its behavior. In fact, by limiting the potentially positive impact of outside influences, containment is likely to do more harm than good. Persisting with this unpopular policy will generate significant friction with American allies in Japan and Europe. But without their support, the attempt to isolate Iran will never succeed.

If the administration chooses to move away from containment and pursue moderate engagement, it could do so in a number of ways. The United States could seek cooperation with Iran on one of several limited issues, such as the efffort to stop narcotics trafficking. In the last decade, Iran has taken several thousand casualties in battles with drug traffickers along its eastern frontier and has requested assistance from the international community. Even without creating formal diplomatic ties, the United States could help out indirectly through the United Nations Drug Control Program. In addition, Washington could support American nongovernmental organizations (NGOs) that could provide humanitarian assistance to the two million Afghan and Iraqi refugees now living in Iran. According to the U.N. High Commissioner for Refugees, Iran today hosts the largest refugee population in the world. This large influx has strained Iran's resources and created social tensions that U.S. aid could help alleviate.

In a similar vein, the Bush administration could also order the Treasury Department's Office of Foreign Assets Control to issue new regulations that would modify the sanctions, permitting limited support by American NGOs for academic, cultural, and civic activities in Iran. This step would remove much of the red tape that currently prevents one of the greatest assets of American democracy—a vibrant nonprofit, nongovernmental sector—from coming to the aid of Iran's emerging but still fragile civil society. In the absence of formal ties, unofficial contacts between NGOs can prove invaluable, laying the groundwork for future relations.

To help lower tensions, the administration could curtail or stop requiring the fingerprinting of the thousands of Iranians who visit the United States each year, and use alternate means to address its security concerns. The blanket regulation on fingerprinting has led to a number of embarrassing episodes that have impeded people-to-people contacts between the two countries and damaged the prospect of an overall improvement in relations.

Washington could also end its active opposition to World Bank lending to Tehran. As it is, the United States seems to be losing this battle: last year, it was rebuffed by other industrialized nations when the bank resumed lending to Iran for public health and sewer projects. The United States also could permit Iran to begin negotiations to join the World Trade Organization. WTO membership would force Iran to make fundamental changes to its economy, especially the vast government-controlled sector, which would improve transparency and bolster the reform movement.

As outlined above, moderate engagement would consist of apparently modest steps. But even these measures would have a high political price and would generate significant bureaucratic opposition within Washington. The State Department designates Iran as a state sponsor of terrorism, and this stigma would make any engagement difficult. To move forward, the Bush administration would have to overcome serious resistance not only within the executive branch but also on Capitol Hill—even though none of these steps would require new legislation. The political costs to the president would be manageable, but they would require careful handling nonetheless.

Of course, the Bush administration could decide that moderate engagement does not go far enough. In that case, Washington could take more dramatic steps toward dismantling U.S. sanctions. The administration could start by permitting U.S. businesses to enter into agreements with Iranian counterparts pending the lifting of sanctions, or it could permit U.S. oil companies to engage in swaps—a mechanism by which oil from the Caspian Basin would be delivered to Northern Iran while an equivalent amount of Iranian oil was shipped out of the south.

A more comprehensive approach would be to lift the ban on all non-military-related U.S. exports, Iranian exports, and U.S. investment in a single, dramatic gesture. Such a bold move could lead to a peculiar kind of relationship that reportedly has already been mooted by high-ranking Iranians: "relations without negotiations." Under this approach, Washington would defer discussions on its areas of concern until after formal diplomatic relations had been established. Some Iranians have interpreted a 1998 statement attributed to the Supreme Leader, Ayatollah Ali Khamenei, that "negotiations are worse than relations" as supportive of this kind of approach.

The administration could also try to prevent the renewal of the Iran-Libya Sanctions Act (ILSA) when it expires in August. ILSA mandates sanctions on foreign firms that invest more than $20 million in Iran's oil and gas sector. This law is symbolically important to Iran, but in practice it does more damage to U.S. relations with Europe, which objects strongly to Washington's attempt to control its allies' behavior. Nonetheless, given the strong support for ILSA in Congress, Bush should not waste political capital fighting its renewal. Instead, he should agree to ILSA's renewal in exchange for congressional support for other Iran-related measures.

In general, however, dropping sanctions on Iran would not be easy and the Bush administration would have a hard time finding support in Congress for such moves. To make matters worse, Iran would probably continue its objectionable policies despite the U.S. overtures. There is a real danger that Iran would refuse to respond in any way, leaving the Bush administration looking naive. For the time being, therefore, moderate engagement is a far safer approach to take.

DETAILS, DETAILS

OVERCOMING so many years of enmity will be extremely difficult. Powerful emotional, structural, and political barriers stand in the way of improved U.S.-Iranian ties—the cumulative result of reported CIA involvement in Prime Minister Mohammad Mossadeq's removal in the 1953 coup, of Washington's support for the repressive and unpopular shah, of the Iranian seizure of American diplomats in 1979, of the U.S. tilt toward Iraq during the Iran-Iraq War of the 1980s, and of the casualties inflicted by Iranian-supported terrorism.

Although many in both governments recognize the need for a better relationship, therefore, widespread hostility in each country remains a serious obstacle. Two examples illustrate this point and highlight the difficulty in moving forward. In September 1999, Iranian Foreign Minister Kamal Kharrazi addressed a gathering on the sidelines of the U.N. General Assembly, where he was asked how Iran would respond if the United States dropped its sanctions on the import of Iranian food and carpets. Kharrazi's prepared answer, carefully noted by U.S. policymakers, declared that Iran would "respond positively" to such a move. In due course, Albright announced six months later the removal of such restrictions. But the positive response promised by Kharrazi never materialized, apparently due to the opposition of Ayatollah Khamenei.

A second example also involves the Albright speech. In her statement, the secretary of state pledged to "explore ways to remove unnecessary impediments to increased contact between Iranian and American scholars, professionals, artists, athletes, and nongovernmental organizations." But the Treasury Department's Office of

Foreign Assets Control, which is charged with sanctions implementation, dragged its feet and delayed granting a general license to permit American NGOs to start supporting their counterparts in Iran until President Clinton left office. As this suggests, governments in both countries may sometimes find it difficult to overcome opposition to improved ties from within their own bureaucracies.

Achieving better relations between the United States and Iran will require building a domestic consensus and overcoming a severe lack of trust. Decision-makers currently fear bold gestures because they worry that their risky steps will not be reciprocated. This problem appears to be even more acute in Iran than in the United States, where many have accepted the arguments for improving ties. Even as Congress remains deeply concerned about Iran's WMD and missile activities, staunch anti-Israel posture, human rights abuses, and support for terrorism, a growing number of legislators have expressed interest in improving relations and in visiting Iran (but have been unable to obtain visas). U.S. businesses, especially oil companies, are nervously watching foreign competitors acquire a foothold in the Iranian market and are loudly advocating a thaw in relations.

Although a strong majority of Iranians also favors improved ties, Ayatollah Khamenei, who under the constitution has the final word on all matters, remains opposed to the idea. Khamenei is sensitive to the opinions of the conservative clergy and the security services, which are his primary sources of support. Thus he has consistently rejected any dialogue with the United States. Khamenei has permitted limited indirect contacts and left the door open to the resumption of commercial ties that would benefit Iran. But he has no interest in working out reciprocal steps that both sides could take to restore confidence and eventually normalize relations.

As Khamenei and his conservative supporters see it, the United States is arrogantly trying to dictate terms to Iran. Given the strong nationalist current in the Iranian psyche and the centrality of "independence" as a core principle of the Islamic Revolution, Iran is particularly sensitive to the notion that sanctions are being used as leverage to effect changes in its behavior. As long as the hated sanctions remain in place, many in Iran will view any dialogue as tantamount to a capitulation to U.S. dictates.

As a result, Iranian diplomats have insisted that in order for relations to improve, the United States must show its respect for Iran's "dignity and honor" by first lifting all sanctions, settling billions of dollars in outstanding legal claims, and dropping its opposition to Iran's serving as a transit route for oil from the Caspian basin. These three conditions seem to reflect a consensus position among Iran's political factions. Even those within Iran who would like to go beyond a commercial relationship and establish political ties have lined up behind this policy in the hope that bringing an end to U.S. sanctions will strengthen their bargaining position on the question of formal relations. And the recent election is unlikely to change any of this.

The positions of the two governments, then, can be summed up as follows. Washington tells Tehran, "let's talk, and when we talk we can discuss sanctions." Tehran replies, "you lift sanctions, and we'll think about talking." Meanwhile, neither side believes that its moves will be reciprocated by the other.

In addition, both sides tend to downplay the importance of developing a new relationship. Iranians feel that U.S. ties have grown less important because of their improving relations with Europe, Japan, Russia, China, and regional players such as Saudi Arabia. Tehran is also convinced that Washington's thirst for oil will eventually bring it around. The United States, on the other hand, seems to feel it has little reason to engage an intermittently hostile, medium-sized country.

Although both countries could survive without improving their relations—indeed, they have managed to do so for more than two decades—neither should miss the opportunity to bolster regional and global security. Negotiations between the two sides might be difficult, but the absence of direct dialogue is worse, since it leads each side to badly misjudge the other's intentions and to misread the other's signals.

UNLIKELY ALLIES

IN LIGHT OF these many factors—U.S. domestic political constraints, the uncertainties surrounding the pace of political evolution in Iran, and the international unpopularity of containment—moderate engagement emerges as the most sensible policy. Washington should make important but limited gestures toward Iran while offering to go much further if Iran reciprocates. Even if the Bush administration does decide to pursue this policy, however, it should have realistic expectations about the troubles ahead. Both sides have already suffered too much from frustrated expectations of the other.

Washington should not expect Tehran to end its more objectionable policies anytime soon—certainly not as a direct response to U.S. overtures. Even with the international community pressuring Iran, it is unlikely to moderate its stance unless its national interests compel it to. Thus Iran is unlikely to withdraw its support for terrorist groups such as Hezbollah or Hamas, which oppose peace in the Middle East, until a comprehensive settlement is struck that sidelines Palestinian radicals and causes Syria to ask Iran to withdraw from the scene. Likewise, Tehran is unlikely to rein in its WMD programs without broad regional talks on the subject and the promise of a safer neighborhood. After all, Iran has had good reason to fear one of its neighbors in particular: Iraq, which has used chemical weapons against Iran in the past.

Given these realities, the Bush administration must separate the question of restoring political ties from the objective of encouraging Iran's moderation and integration as a responsible member of the international community. The latter can be achieved without the former and is so important to U.S. interests that it is worth pursuing on its own.

Moderate engagement would encourage Iran's collaboration with multilateral institutions, help its integration with the global trading system, and give it far stronger incentives to improve its behavior than has the containment policy. Moderate engagement would also bring the United States into closer alignment with its allies, decreasing friction and improving the chances for a more effective common approach.

Meanwhile, moderate engagement would begin a gradual process of laying the groundwork for an eventual rapprochement once Iran's domestic political situation permits it to move forward. Many Iranians now recognize that the best way to secure their country's future is by making a positive contribution to international peace and security. A new U.S. policy would strengthen their hand, helping them do just that.●

The Rogue Who Came in From the Cold

Ray Takeyh

LIBYA MENDS ITS WAYS

As THE Bush administration struggles to define its foreign policy, with sanctions slipping on Iraq and the prospect of missile defense raising complications around the world, a new question has emerged: How should Washington handle a "rogue" state that is gradually abandoning its objectionable practices? What should the United States do when its long-standing policy toward a maverick country such as Libya starts to pay off—and that country finally begins to clean up its act? The question has recently become a pressing one as, in a surprising twist of events, the often and justifiably maligned Libyan regime of Colonel Mu'ammar Qaddafi has started to meet international demands and redress its past crimes. How the United States responds will serve as a test of Washington's ability to reintegrate a reforming "rogue" into the community of nations.

On January 31, three Scottish judges deliberating at a specially convened court in the Netherlands convicted a Libyan intelligence agent for the 1988 bombing of Pan Am flight 103. The attack, which occurred over Lockerbie, Scotland, killed 270 passengers (including 189 Americans) and passersby, dramatizing the threat that terrorism and its state sponsors pose to the United States. The recent verdict has achieved a modicum of justice. But it has only reconfirmed, rather than resolved, the quandary that Libya's behav-

---

RAY TAKEYH is a former Soref Research Fellow at the Washington Institute for Near East Policy.

ior raises for U.S. foreign policy. On the one hand, the verdict seems to have validated long-held perceptions of Libya as a pariah state. But on the other hand, the very fact that Qaddafi surrendered the suspects suggests that international pressure has prompted subtle yet significant changes in his foreign policy. After decades of militancy, Libya seems to be accommodating itself to international norms.

Few have acknowledged the true dimensions of the challenge these changes pose for Washington. President George W. Bush must deal with the remaining Lockerbie-related issues—including how to force Tripoli to accept responsibility for the crime—while also figuring out how to move beyond them. Successive American administrations have proven adept at devising strategies for isolating offending regimes such as Libya's. But Washington has thus far neglected to plan what to do when it succeeds.

RADICAL SHEIK

Mu'ammar Qaddafi came of age during the 1960s, as Libya and much of the developing world battled to escape imperial domination. This bitter struggle against colonialism shaped Qaddafi's political philosophy, infusing him with a deep suspicion of the West. It also convinced him of the inherent iniquity of the international order, and led him to the conclusion that Tripoli should be unfettered by international conventions or rules. Rather, as a vanguard revolutionary state, Libya should help liberate the rest of the Third World and reshape its political institutions.

With Libya's vast oil wealth at his disposal and a radical ideology as his guide, Qaddafi systematically attacked Western—especially American—interests, as well as conservative African and Arab leaders whom he routinely derided as "lackeys of imperialism." Libya lent its support to liberation movements, secessionists, and terrorists from the Philippines to Argentina, embarking on a course that culminated in the Pan Am explosion.

Then, in the 1990s, certain events pressed Qaddafi toward a pragmatic redefinition of his nation's interests. The collapse of the Soviet Union deprived Libya of its main counterweight to the

United States and exposed it to the kind of unified international pressure that was once impossible. As Qaddafi became isolated, his ideology and methods came to seem hopelessly anachronistic. The colonel's anti-imperialism was eclipsed as the nonaligned bloc turned its attention to securing its position in the global economy. While Qaddafi remained rigid, much of the rest of the Arab world came to terms with Israel and grudgingly accepted the need for an American security umbrella. Libya's continuous interference in the internal affairs of other African states, meanwhile, estranged Qaddafi from that continent, the liberation of which he had often trumpeted as one of his highest priorities. Qaddafi thus spent the 1990s on the sidelines while his onetime revolutionary compatriots—leaders such as Nelson Mandela and Yasir Arafat—were feted in Washington and in European capitals. To remain relevant, Qaddafi realized, he had to accept the passing of the age of revolutions and the arrival of the age of globalization.

Another reason for Qaddafi's shift was the much-derided U.N. sanctions regime imposed on Libya after the Lockerbie bombing. The colonel had long believed that Libya's oil wealth and commercial appeal would undermine any cohesive opposition to his revolutionary excesses. But the Lockerbie sanctions, enacted by the United Nations in 1992, shattered that conviction. The United States managed to convince even states with close economic ties to Libya, such as Italy and Germany, to support the sanctions as a way to force Qaddafi to hand over the bombing suspects. As a senior Libyan official admitted, "when America imposed an embargo, the whole world followed it." For the first time, Qaddafi's militancy incurred a palpable cost.

Prior attempts to coerce Libya had proven ineffective: U.S. air strikes in 1986 only enhanced Qaddafi's domestic power and led to his lionization in the developing world. But the U.N. sanctions—particularly the prohibition on the sale of oil equipment and technology and a ban on financial transfers—hit Qaddafi where it hurt the most, undermining his government's ability to extract and export its main source of revenue. Libya estimates that the sanctions have deprived its economy of $33 billion, whereas the World Bank puts the damage at the lower but still daunting sum of $18 billion. Whatever their actual cost, the basic efficacy of the sanctions demonstrated Libya's special vulnerability to such multilateral coercion. Libya's economic vitality and its government's popularity depend on access to international petroleum markets. Thus the same resource that gave Qaddafi the power to upset the international order also let the world community undermine him.

Already, in the 1980s, low oil prices had sparked an economic recession from which Libya could not escape. The sanctions of the 1990s then exacerbated the woes of an economy that was plagued with 30 percent unemployment and 50 percent inflation rates. Tripoli embarked on an austerity program, freezing salaries and reducing subsidies, but this proved dangerous for a regime that depended for its survival on buying the population's acquiescence. Demonstrations in urban areas soon erupted, as did at least two military coup attempts and an Islamic insurgency in the eastern provinces.

As Libya approached the brink of chaos in the mid-1990s, an extraordinary dispute broke out in the higher echelons of the regime. The pragmatists in the bureaucracy—led by the late General Secretary Umar al-Muntasir and Energy Minister Abdallah Salim al-Badri—stressed the need for structural economic reforms and international investments to ensure Libya's long-term economic vitality and political stability. The hard-liners—including long-time Qaddafi confidant Abdelssalem Jalloud—wanted to continue defying the West, for they saw Libya's past radicalism as the basis of the regime's legitimacy.

As the debate raged, Qaddafi at first remained strangely silent, unwilling or unable to make a decision. But in 1998, the colonel seemed to resolve the debate in favor of the pragmatists. A series of articles in the official daily *Al-Jamahiriya* began to criticize the intransigence of the hard-liners and their inability to recognize prevailing global realities. The Revolutionary Committees—informal groups of zealots, drawn from the lower echelons of Libyan society and indoctrinated in radical ideology, that served as the hard-liners' power base and had dominated Libyan politics since their creation in the late 1970s—were purged and relegated to the margins of society. Meanwhile, the pragmatists were granted an all-important advantage: proximity to the colonel. "We cannot stand in the way of progress," announced Qaddafi. "No more obstacles between human beings are accepted. The fashion now is the free market and investments." In April 1999, Qaddafi accepted U.N. demands for the trial of the Lockerbie suspects in the Netherlands, announcing shortly thereafter that "the world has changed radically and drastically. The methods and ideas should change, and being a revolutionary and a progressive man, I have to follow this movement."

In the last few years, Qaddafi has begun to offer a new vision for Libya. In a September 2000 speech commemorating the Libyan Revolution, he not only proclaimed an end to his long-standing anti-imperialist struggle but also suggested that it was time for former antagonists to start cooperating with one another. In a series of seminars and speeches, the colonel outlined his new ideas to his restive constituents, declaring, "Now is the era of economy, consumption, markets, and investments. This is what unites people irrespective of language, religion, and nationalities." The hoary policies of subsidizing rebellions and plotting the overthrow of sovereign leaders have become unsustainable in the era of economic interdependence—even for oil-rich Libya. As a sign of the times, the regular procession of visitors to the colonel's tent no longer includes guerrilla leaders and terrorists, but instead features investment consultants and Internet executives.

Qaddafi has also begun to shift his international focus toward Africa. After decades of involvement in the Middle East, in March 1999 the colonel proclaimed his new orientation with a typical flourish, announcing, "I have no time to lose talking with Arabs. ... I now talk about Pan-Africanism and African unity." There is a certain logic to this new focus; after all, the Organization of African Unity (OAU) was the only regional group to defy the U.N. sanctions on Libya, and Nelson Mandela, Africa's elder statesman, was instrumental in resolving the Lockerbie crisis. While Arab politicians equivocated during the 1990s, African leaders warmly embraced Qaddafi. Mandela even hailed him as "one of the revolutionary icons of our time."

Libya's new Africa policy has become the first test of Qaddafi's evolving ideology and newfound moderation. Previously, Libya had tried to export revolution through Africa by subsidizing insurgencies and destabilizing local states. Now Qaddafi seems to have abandoned his radical heritage. He has focused on mediating crises while claiming a place at the African roundtable. The colonel has embarked on a high-profile diplomatic campaign to settle conflicts in the Democratic Republic of the Congo, the Horn of Africa, Sudan, and Sierra Leone. Libya has also signed bilateral trade and cultural pacts with Niger, Senegal, and South Africa, while extending aid to Ethiopia, the Ivory Coast, Mali, Tanzania, Uganda, and Zimbabwe. Tripoli has even demonstrated an uncharacteristic appreciation for multilateral institutions. Not only has it participated constructively in various regional forums, but it has hosted an extraordinary OAU meeting to press for the creation of a "United States of Africa" as a means to promote solidarity and economic integration. Most of these initiatives have yet to produce substantial practical results. But their importance lies in the fact that, after decades of attempting to subvert Africa's state system, Qaddafi is now making positive contributions to the continent's political cohesion and economic rehabilitation.

THE ROAD TO REDEMPTION

QADDAFI's philosophical evolution and his African endeavors have sparked some interest in the international community. But further changes must occur before rapprochement with the United States will be possible. Three problems in particular loom large: Libya's support for terrorism, its attempts to acquire weapons of mass destruction (WMD), and its opposition to the Arab-Israeli peace process.

American objectives in Libya have never been explicitly directed at toppling Qaddafi. This is explained by the fact that the colonel's adventurism, while disturbing to Americans, has never actually destabilized fundamental U.S. interests. This puts Qaddafi in a very different category from that occupied by a leader like Saddam Hussein, who twice invaded his neighbors and continues to seek hegemony over the Persian Gulf. Qaddafi has also shown himself to be more susceptible to international pressure than

Saddam. Successive American administrations have stated that they would welcome resumed relations with Libya if Qaddafi would just abandon his provocative behavior. Now he may finally be doing just that.

Although Libya has a long history of supporting outlawed organizations such as Italy's Red Brigades and the Irish Republican Army, Qaddafi has recently severed his links to his terrorist clients and abandoned terrorism as an instrument of policy. In 1999, for example, Libya expelled the Abu Nidal organization from its territory and broke its ties to other radical Palestinian groups such as the Popular Front for Liberation of Palestine–General Command and Palestinian Islamic Jihad. In addition, in accordance with an Arab League agreement, Libya has extradited Islamist militants and suspected terrorists to Egypt, Yemen, and Jordan. Once-notorious training camps have been closed down, and terror groups have been told to find other sources of arms and supplies.

Apart from terrorism, U.S. policymakers have also been concerned by Libya's attempts to acquire WMD. Here there seem to be fewer signs of improvement. Since the April 1999 suspension of the U.N. arms embargo, Libya has sought to modernize its decrepit armed forces by acquiring advanced weapons from North Korea and Russia. And the CIA recently announced that "Tripoli has not given up its goal of establishing its own offensive [chemical weapons] program."

Although Libya has made progress toward acquiring chemical weapons, it has not yet managed to become a nuclear threat. As the Pentagon describes it, Libya's nuclear project "lacks well-developed plans, expertise, consistent financial support, and adequate foreign suppliers." And Libya's nuclear infrastructure is limited to a Soviet-made research reactor operating under the auspices of the International Atomic Energy Agency.

Washington should recognize that Tripoli's attempts to acquire WMD make a certain kind of sense. After all, Libya is richer than its neighbors but is sparsely populated and has long, unsettled borders. The country's lucrative oil fields have, at various times, been coveted by neighbors such as Algeria. And Libya's unsteady relations with Egypt have caused sporadic tension on Libya's eastern flank. Little wonder, then, that Tripoli has chosen to build up its air power, missile force, and chemical weapons in order to deter potential adversaries with larger armies. Both of these factors—the rudimentary level of Libya's WMD program and the genuine basis for its regional insecurity—suggest that it might be possible to persuade Tripoli to abandon its plans for WMD. U.S. diplomacy should persuade Libya that its WMD projects will only precipitate a regional arms race that will exacerbate, rather than alleviate, its vulnerability. Even if Qaddafi remains unpersuaded, Libya's primitive facilities and poor technological infrastructure ensure that the country will not become a nuclear threat anytime soon.

A third major obstacle in U.S.-Libyan relations has been Qaddafi's ferocious rejection of efforts to settle the conflict between Israel and its neighbors. But here again Libya seems to have undergone a conversion in the past few years. Although the colonel still makes shrill calls for the "battle of the century" to end the "Zionist occupation," on a practical level Libya has yielded to American demands by terminating its support for rejectionist Palestinian groups and accepting the Palestinian Authority's right to negotiate with Israel. In the past, the kind of violence now occurring in the West Bank and Gaza would have led to the dispatch of Libyan arms and aid to Palestinian militants. This time, Qaddafi has limited himself to sporadic rhetorical fulmination and avoided tangible measures that would add further strain to an already tense situation. Qaddafi may never cross the existential barrier that some other Arab leaders have traversed by recognizing Israel. But in practice, he has already extricated Libya from Arab-Israeli confrontations.

Libya's ongoing reintegration into the world community has already started to pay off, and the rewards it has won from reclaimed trade partnerships have generated a desire within the country to come to terms with the Americans as well. Unlike Iran, which refuses official contact with the United States, Libya is eager to open a diplomatic dialogue. Abuzed Dorda, Libya's U.N. envoy, has said, "I expect that we will sit down with the Americans and put the past behind us." Even Qaddafi, in his own eccentric manner, has made overtures to the new American president, stressing, "I believe that George W. Bush will be nice. As a person he is not malicious or imperialist. I believe that he attaches importance to the United States and does not have world ambitions." A modest level of trade has already quietly developed between the two states. Last year, Libya took advantage of the newly eased sanctions on food and medicine to purchase 50,500 tons of wheat and 26,100 tons of corn from the United States. In a further, subtle signal to the United States, last November Libyan General Secretary Mubarak al-Shamikh dismissed reports that U.S. oil companies' assets in Libya have been nationalized and pledged that American investments are "protected and waiting for them to return." All of this suggests that a flexible yet determined American policy toward Libya stands a good chance of convincing Qaddafi to make further pragmatic adjustments.

NEW WINE IN NEW BOTTLES

THE CHALLENGE that Libya poses for the Bush administration is how to acknowledge Qaddafi's partial rehabilitation while continuing to press for further changes. Until now, the United States has relied on a range of unilateral and coercive measures (such as sanctions) to contain Libya. But in the aftermath of the Lockerbie trial, with U.N. sanctions having been suspended, the United States can hardly isolate Libya on its own. Unless it adds incentives to the mix, Washington will have little in the way of leverage.

Unlike the United States, Europe has responded to Libya's overtures with uncritical dialogue and greatly increased trade. But whereas U.S. policy may be too unyielding, the European model goes too far in the other direction. By warmly welcoming Libya back into the international fold, Europe has rewarded (or, at best, ignored) Qaddafi's continued refusal to accept basic responsibility for the Pan Am bombing and turned a blind eye to his noncompliance with other international demands. Still, since Europe is Libya's foremost trading partner and the market for nine-tenths of its oil exports, the success of any U.S. policy will depend on European compliance and support.

A U.S.-Libyan dialogue should start by focusing on the remaining U.N. demands relating to Lockerbie—namely, that Tripoli pay compensation to the families of the victims and formally renounce terrorism. For symbolic reasons and to deter future crimes, these two points should be made non-negotiable prerequisites to any softening of U.S. policy toward Libya. Fortunately, the chances for success on these issues are good. Despite Libya's refusal to compensate Americans for state-sponsored crimes, recent history suggests it may eventually offer restitution. In 1999, for example, after a court in France convicted six Libyan intelligence officials for the 1989 bombing of a French UTA flight over West Africa, Libya paid out $25.7 million in reparations. Now, in exchange for both direct compensation and a Libyan admission of responsibility, Washington should consider removing Tripoli from its list of state sponsors of terrorism, rescinding its ban on American citizens' travel to Libya, and unfreezing the country's assets in the United States.

A similar approach should be used to dissuade Libya from acquiring WMD. The chances that Libya will manage to assemble nuclear weapons anytime soon are remote, but Qaddafi's pursuit of chemical weapons and delivery systems remains a threat. The United States should therefore mount a concerted diplomatic campaign involving not just Libya but also Europe. The political cost of the five-year-old Iran-Libya Sanctions Act (ILSA) has been considerable and its impact on deterring investments in "rogue" states negligible. The Bush administration should thus allow ILSA to expire in August in exchange for a European ban on the export to Libya of sensitive technology.

In a similar vein, the United States should start talking to Russia about preventing arms sales to Libya. Since these sales have been stymied by long-outstanding Libyan debts for prior purchases, the Russians may be more inclined to cooperate here than they have been on arms sales to Iran. In the end, however, keeping WMD technology out of Libyan hands will require a complex, broad-based, and multilateral policy.

In addition to coordinating international measures, the United States should also use its own set of incentives to get Tripoli to acquiesce to various WMD treaties. Libya has already signed the nuclear Nonproliferation Treaty. It should be pressed to sign the

Chemical Weapons Convention as well, and to permit the inspections that treaty mandates. In exchange for such compliance, the United States could stop blocking Libya's access to international capital markets, establish low-level diplomatic representation, and allow U.S. investment in Libya's non-oil sectors. The flow of investments into Libya need not be limited to the energy sector: Tripoli is also trying to refurbish its airline and financial services industries and its national infrastructure, and these projects offer lucrative opportunities for U.S. firms.

RIGHTING THE ROGUE

IT MAY TAKE a number of years before U.S.-Libyan diplomatic relations are fully restored at the ambassadorial level and American oil firms return to Libya. Until then, the United States should monitor Libya's compliance with international standards and offer concessions only after judging Tripoli's record. The current administration should aim simply to establish a framework that can be used for the gradual resumption of U.S.-Libyan ties.

American policy, furthermore, should not try to directly alter Libya's international orientation. Instead, it should provide various inducements and pressures designed to help Libya move along its own path of moderation. This incremental normalization would reward constructive Libyan conduct and punish intransigence. It would also have the advantage of reconstituting international—particularly European—cooperation, an essential part of any Libya policy.

Most important, the Bush administration ought to accept the possibility of "rogue" states' rehabilitation. U.S. policy should employ a full complement of economic, political, and diplomatic tools not just to frustrate these states' nefarious designs but also to show them that, should they temper their policies, they can be reintegrated into global society. The Libyan case can provide a model for how to deal with a revolutionary regime that has grown weary of its isolation and ostracism. The United States should not waste the opportunity. Libya—and the world—will be watching.✪

The Future of
Political Islam

Graham E. Fuller

IT'S NOT OVER 'TIL IT'S OVER

WERE THE ATTACKS of September 11, 2001, the final gasp of Islamic radicalism or the opening salvo of a more violent confrontation between Muslim extremists and the West? And what does the current crisis imply for the future of the Islamic world itself? Will Muslims recoil from the violence and sweeping anti-Westernism unleashed in their name, or will they allow Osama bin Laden and his cohort to shape the character of future relations between Muslims and the West?

The answers to these questions lie partly in the hands of the Bush administration. The war on terrorism has already dealt a major blow to the personnel, infrastructure, and operations of bin Laden's al Qaeda network. Just as important, it has burst the bubble of euphoria and sense of invincibility among radical Islamists that arose from the successful jihad against the Soviet occupation of Afghanistan. But it is not yet clear whether the war will ultimately alleviate or merely exacerbate the current tensions in the Muslim world.

Depending on one's perspective, the attacks on the World Trade Center and the Pentagon can be seen either as a success, evidence that a few activists can deal a grievous blow to a superpower in the name of their cause, or as a failure, since the attackers brought on the demise of their state sponsor and most likely of their own organization while galvanizing nearly global opposition.

GRAHAM E. FULLER is former Vice-Chairman of the National Intelligence Council at the CIA and is finishing a new book on Islamism.

To help the latter lesson triumph, the United States will have to move beyond the war's first phase, which has punished those directly responsible for the attacks, and address the deeper sources of political violence and terror in the Muslim world today.

THE MANY FACES OF ISLAMISM

PRESIDENT BUSH has repeatedly stressed that the war on terrorism is not a war on Islam. But by seeking to separate Islam from politics, the West ignores the reality that the two are intricately intertwined across a broad swath of the globe from northern Africa to Southeast Asia. Transforming the Muslim environment is not merely a matter of rewriting school textbooks or demanding a less anti-Western press. The simple fact is that political Islam, or Islamism—defined broadly as the belief that the Koran and the Hadith (Traditions of the Prophet's life) have something important to say about the way society and governance should be ordered—remains the most powerful ideological force in that part of the world.

The Islamist phenomenon is hardly uniform, however; multiple forms of it are spreading, evolving, and diversifying. Today one encounters Islamists who may be either radical or moderate, political or apolitical, violent or quietist, traditional or modernist, democratic or authoritarian. The oppressive Taliban of Afghanistan and the murderous Algerian Armed Islamic Group (known by its French acronym, GIA) lie at one fanatic point of a compass that also includes Pakistan's peaceful and apolitical preaching-to-the-people movement, the Tablighi Jamaat; Egypt's mainstream conservative parliamentary party, the Muslim Brotherhood; and Turkey's democratic and modernist Fazilet/Ak Party.

Turkey's apolitical Nur movement embraces all aspects of science as compatible with Islam because secular scientific knowledge reinforces the wonder of God's world. Indonesia's syncretic Nahdatul Ulama eschews any Islamic state at all in its quest to further appreciation of God's role in human life. Islamist feminist movements are studying the Koran and Islamic law (the *shari`a*) in order to interpret the teachings for themselves and distinguish between what their religion clearly stipulates and those traditions arbitrarily devised and enforced by patriarchal leaders (such as mandatory head-to-toe covering or the ban on female driving in Saudi Arabia). These are but a few among the vast array of movements that work in the media, manage Web sites, conduct massive welfare programs, run schools and hospitals, represent flourishing Muslim nongovernmental organizations, and exert a major impact on Muslim life.

Islamism has become, in fact, the primary vehicle and vocabulary of most political discourse throughout the Muslim world. When Westerners talk about political ideals, they naturally hark back to the Magna Carta, the American Revolution, and the French Revolution. Muslims go back to the Koran and the Hadith to derive general principles about good governance (including the ruler's obligation to consult the people) and concepts of social and economic justice. Neither Islam nor Islamism says much about concrete state institutions, and frankly nobody knows exactly what a modern Islamic state should look like—since few have ever existed and none provides a good model. But Islamists today use general Islamic ideals as a touchstone for criticizing, attacking, or even trying to overthrow what are perceived as authoritarian, corrupt, incompetent, and illegitimate regimes.

No other ideology has remotely comparable sway in the Muslim world. The region's nationalist parties are weak and discredited, and nationalism itself has often been absorbed into Islamism; the left is marginalized and in disarray; liberal democrats cannot even muster enough supporters to stage a demonstration in any Muslim capital. Like it or not, therefore, various forms of Islamism will be the dominant intellectual current in the region for some time to come—and the process is still in its infancy. In the end, modern liberal governance is more likely to take root through organically evolving liberal Islamist trends at the grassroots level than from imported Western modules of "instant democracy."

A DYNAMIC PHENOMENON

MOST WESTERN OBSERVERS tend to look at the phenomenon of political Islam as if it were a butterfly in a collection box, captured and skewered for eternity, or as a set of texts unbendingly prescribing a single path. This is why some scholars who examine its core writings proclaim Islam to be incompatible with democracy—as if any religion in its origins was about democracy at all.

Such observers have the question wrong. The real issue is not what Islam is, but what Muslims want. People of all sorts of faiths can rapidly develop interpretations of their religion that justify practically any political quest. This process, moreover, is already underway among Muslims. Contemporary Islam is a dynamic phenomenon. It includes not only bin Laden and the Taliban, but also liberals who are clearly embarking on their own Reformation with potentially powerful long-term consequences. Deeply entrenched traditionalists find these latter stirrings a threat, but many more Muslims, including many Islamists, see such efforts to understand eternal values in contemporary terms as essential to a living faith.

Regrettably, until recently Islam had been living (with striking periodic exceptions) in a state of intellectual stagnation for many hundreds of years. Western colonizers further vitiated and marginalized Islamic thought and institutions, and postindependence leadership has done no better, tending to draw on quasi-fascist Western models of authoritarian control. Only now is Islam emerging into a period of renewed creativity, freedom, and independence. Much of this new activity, ironically, is occurring in the freedom of the West, where dozens of Islamic institutes are developing new ideas and employing modern communications to spur debate and disseminate information.

The process of diversification and evolution within modern Islamism is driven by multiple internal forces, but these developments are always ultimately contingent on the tolerance of local regimes, the nature of local politics, and the reigning pattern of global power. Most regimes see almost any form of political Islam as a threat, since it embodies a major challenge to their unpopular, failing, and illegitimate presidents-for-life or isolated monarchs. How the regime responds to the phenomenon often plays a major role in determining how the local Islamist movement develops.

Does the regime permit elections and free political discussion? How repressive is it, and how violent is the political culture in which it operates? How do existing economic and social conditions affect the political process? The answers to these questions go a long way toward describing how Islamists—like all other political actors—will behave in any particular country. That said, these days nearly all Islamists push hard for democracy, believing that they will benefit from it and flourish within it. They also have discovered the importance of human rights—at least in the political field—precisely because they are usually the primary victims of the absence of rights, filling regional jails in disproportionate numbers.

Some skepticism is due, of course, about the ability of Islamists to run effective and moderate governments, especially when the three Islamic state models to date—Iran, Sudan, and the Taliban's Afghanistan—have all failed dramatically in this area. Only Iran has lately shown signs of exciting evolution within an Islamic framework. But it is worth recalling that all of those regimes came to power by social revolution, military coup, or civil war, virtually guaranteeing continuing despotism regardless of which party was in charge.

The true test of any Islamist party comes when it gains office by the ballot box and must then adhere while in power to the democratic norms it touted in opposition. History unfortunately gives few precedents here. Turkey's brief experience under an elected Islamist-led coalition comes closest, but the government was removed by the military after a year of mixed performance, leaving the experiment unfinished. Secular Turks continue to elect Islamist mayors in major cities across the country, however, including Istanbul and Ankara, because they deliver what constituents want.

Americans brought up to venerate the separation of church and state may wonder whether a movement with an explicit religious vision can ever create a democratic, tolerant, and pluralistic polity. But if Christian Democrats can do it, there is no reason in principle why Islamists cannot. This is what the cleric President Mohammed Khatami is trying to achieve in Iran, in fact, although his efforts are being blocked by a hard-line clerical faction. Non-Muslims should understand that democratic values are latent in Islamic thought if one wants to look for them, and that it would be more natural and organic for the Muslim world to derive contemporary liberal practices from its own sources than to import them wholesale from foreign cultures. The key question is whether it will actually do so.

The Future of Political Islam

WHO'S BESIEGING WHOM?

THE LIBERAL EVOLUTION of political Islam faces some formidable obstacles. The first, as noted, comes from the local political scene, where Islamists are routinely suppressed, jailed, tortured, and executed. Such circumstances encourage the emergence of secret, conspiratorial, and often armed groups rather than liberal ones.

The second obstacle comes from international politics, which often pushes Islamist movements and parties in an unfortunate direction. A familiar phenomenon is the Muslim national liberation movement. In more than a dozen countries, large, oppressed Muslim minorities, who are also ethnically different from their rulers, have sought autonomy or independence—witness the Palestinians, Chechens, Chinese Uighurs, Filipino Moros, and Kashmiris, among others. In these cases, Islam serves to powerfully bolster national liberation struggles by adding a "holy" religious element to an emerging ethnic struggle. These causes have attracted a kind of Muslim "foreign legion" of radicalized, volunteer mujahideen, some of whom have joined al Qaeda.

A third obstacle comes from the Islamists' own long list of grievances against the forces and policies perceived to be holding Muslims back in the contemporary world, many of them associated with liberalism's supposed avatar, the United States. The litany includes U.S. support for authoritarianism in the Muslim world in the name of stability or material interests such as ensuring the flow of oil, routine U.S. backing of Israeli policies, and Washington's failure to press for democratic political processes out of fear that they might bring Islamist groups to power.

Islamists, too, deserve criticism for playing frequently opportunistic political games—like so many other fledgling parties. Where they exist legally, they often adopt radical postures on Islamic issues to embarrass the government. The major Islamist PAS movement in Malaysia, for example—which now governs two of the country's ten states—has called for full implementation of the *shari`a* and application of traditional Muslim punishments (including amputations and stoning), in part to show up the poor Islamic credentials of the central government. In Egypt and Kuwait, meanwhile, Islamist groups regularly call for more conservative social measures, partly to score political points, and have often inhibited the intellectual freedom on Islamic issues which these societies desperately require. Such posturing tends to bid up the level of Islamic strictness within the country in question in a closed atmosphere of Islamic political correctness. Still, most Islamists have quite concrete domestic agendas related to local politics and social issues that are far removed from the transnational, apocalyptic visions of a bin Laden.

Ironically, even as Westerners feel threatened by Islam, most in the Muslim world feel themselves besieged by the West, a reality only dimly grasped in the United States. They see the international order as dramatically skewed against them and their interests, in a world where force and the potential for force dominate the agenda. They are overwhelmed by feelings of political impotence. Muslim rulers fear offending their protectors in Washington, Muslim publics have little or no influence over policy within their own states, bad leaders cannot be changed, and public expression of dissent is punished, often brutally. This is the "stability" in the Middle East to which the United States seems wedded.

Under such conditions, it should not be surprising that these frustrated populations perceive the current war against terrorism as functionally a war against Islam. Muslim countries are the chief target, they contend, Muslims everywhere are singled out for censure and police attention, and U.S. power works its will across the region with little regard for deeper Muslim concerns. A vicious circle exists: dissatisfaction leads to anti-regime action, which leads to repression, which in turn leads to terrorism, U.S. military intervention, and finally further dissatisfaction. Samuel Huntington's theory of a "clash of civilizations" is seemingly vindicated before the Muslim world's eyes.

THEIR MUSLIM PROBLEM—AND OURS

SEVERAL REGIMES have decided to play the dangerous game of trying to "out-Islam the Islamists," embracing harsh social and intellectual interpretations of Islam themselves so as to bolster their credentials against Islamist opposition. Thus in Egypt, the government-controlled University of al-Azhar, a prestigious voice in interpreting Islam, issues its own brand of intolerant fundamentalist rulings; Pakistan does something similar. The issue here is not the actual Islamist agenda but whose Islamist writ will dominate. Islam is simply the vehicle and coinage of the struggle between the state and its challengers.

In a comparable fashion, Islam and Islamist movements today provide a key source of identity to peoples intent on strengthening their social cohesion against Western cultural assault. Religious observance is visibly growing across the region, often accompanied by the "Arabization" of customs in clothing, food, mosque architecture, and ritual—even in areas such as Africa and East Asia, where no such customs had previously existed and where claims to cultural authenticity or tradition are weak to say the least. Association with the broader *umma,* the international Muslim community, is attractive because it creates new bonds of solidarity that can be transformed into increased international clout.

Islam and Islamist concepts, finally, are often recruited into existing geopolitical struggles. In the 1980s, for example, the rivalry between Saudi Arabia and Iran, often cloaked as a simple Sunni versus Shi`a competition, was as much political as it was religious. The Saudis hoped that their puritanical and intolerant Wahhabi vision of Islam would prevail over the Iranian revolutionary vision. For better or worse it did, partly because the Saudis could bankroll movements and schools far outside Saudi borders, and partly because many Sunnis considered Iran's Shi`ism anathema. The radical Islamic groups one sees today in the Philippines, Central Asia, the Caucasus, Afghanistan, and Pakistan, among other places, are partly the fruits of this export of Wahhabism, nourished by local conditions, ideological and material needs, and grievances.

Islam has thus become a vehicle and vocabulary for the expression of many different agendas in the Muslim world. The West is not at war with the religion itself, but it is indeed challenged by the radicalism that some groups have embraced. Muslims may too readily blame the West for their own problems, but their frustrations and current grievances are real. Indeed, the objective indicators of living conditions in the Islamic world—whether political, economic, or social—are generally turning down. Cultures and communities under siege naturally tend to opt for essentialism, seeking comfort and commonality in a back-to-basics view of religion, a narrowing and harshening of cultural and nationalist impulses, and a return to traditional community values. Muslims under pressure today are doing just this, retreating back to the solid certainties of essentialist Islam while their societies are in chaos. When Grozny was flattened by Russian troops, the Chechens declared Islamic law—clinging to an unquestioned traditional moral framework for comfort, familiarity, and reassuring moral discipline.

As a result, even as liberalization is occurring within some Islamist movements, much of the Islamic community is heading in the other direction, growing more austere and less tolerant and modernist. The same harsh conditions produce a quest for heroes, strongmen, and potential saviors. One of the saddest commentaries today, in fact, is the Muslim thirst for heroes who will stand up and defy the dominant U.S.-led order—a quest that has led them to cheer on the Saddam Husseins and bin Ladens of the world.

The Muslim world is therefore in a parlous condition. Some in the West may think that Islam's problem is not their problem, that Muslims just need to face reality and get on with it. But the September 11 attacks showed that in a globalized world, their problems can become our problems. The U.S. tendency to disregard popular Muslim concerns as Washington cooperates with oppressive and insecure regimes fosters an environment in which acts of terrorism become thinkable and, worse, even gratifying in the eyes of the majority. The vast bulk of Muslims, of course, will go no further than to cheer on those who lash out. But such an environment is perhaps the most dangerous of all, because it legitimizes and encourages not the tolerant and liberalizing Islamists and peacemakers, but the negativistic hard-liners and rejectionists.

THE SILENT MUSLIM MAJORITY

FEW MUSLIMS around the world want to inflict endless punishment on the United States or go to war with it. Most of them recognize what happened on September 11 as a monstrous crime. But they still hope that the attacks will serve as a "lesson" to the United States to wake up and change its policies toward the Middle East.

Most would emphatically reject, however, a key contention of President George W. Bush, that those who sympathize with the attacks are people who "hate freedom." Nearly all Muslims worldwide admire and aspire to the same political freedoms that Americans take for granted. A central complaint of theirs, in fact, is that U.S. policies have helped block the freedoms necessary to develop their personal and national capacities in comparable ways.

Muslim societies may have multiple problems, but hating American political values is not among them. U.S. policymakers would be wise to drop this simplistic, inaccurate, and self-serving description of the problem. They should instead consider what steps the United States can take to spread those political values to areas where they have been noticeable chiefly by their absence.

For Muslims who live in the West, the attacks of September 11 posed a moment of self-definition. However acutely attuned they might have been to the grievances of the broader Muslim world, the vast majority recognized that it was Western values and practices with which they identifed most. This reaction suggests there may be a large silent majority in the Islamic world, caught between the powerful forces of harsh and entrenched regimes on the one hand and the inexorable will of an angry superpower on the other. Right now they have few channels of expression between acceptance of a miserable status quo and siding with the world-wreckers' vision of apocalyptic confrontation. How can the United States help mobilize this camp? What can make the members of this silent majority think they are anything but ringside spectators at a patently false clash of civilizations unfolding before their eyes?

Today most moderate Islamists, as well as the few Muslim liberals around, maintain a discouragingly low profile. Although they have condemned the September 11 attacks, they have been reluctant to scrutinize the conditions of their own societies that contribute to these problems. This myopia stems partly from an anxiety about signing on to the sweeping, unpredictable, and open-ended U.S. agenda for its war on terrorism. That said, however, it also stems from a failure of will to preach hard truths when society is under siege.

Given the authoritarian realities of life in the region, what acceptable outlets of expression are available? Islamists and other social leaders should find some way of setting forth a critique of Muslim society that will galvanize a call for change. Even if presidents-for-life cannot be removed, other demands can be made—for better services, more rights, freer economies. It is inexcusable that a Muslim civilization that led the entire world for a thousand years in the arts and sciences today ranks near the bottom of world literacy rates. Although conditions for women vary widely in the Muslim world, overall their levels of education and social engagement are depressingly low—not just a human scandal but also a prime indicator of underdevelopment. When highly traditional or fanatic groups attempt to define Islam in terms of a social order from a distant past, voices should be raised to deny them that monopoly.

The United States, meanwhile, should contribute to this effort by beginning to engage overseas Muslims vigorously, including those Islamic clerics who enjoy great respect and authority as men of uncompromised integrity. Both sides will benefit from a dialogue that initially will reveal deep fissures in thought and approach, but that over time may begin to bridge numerous gaps. Many of these clerics represent undeniably moderate forces within political Islam, but their own understanding of the West, though far from uniformly hostile, is flawed and often initially unsympathetic. They could learn from visits to the United States and dialogue with Americans—if ever they were granted visas.

It is worth noting, however, that this process will be fought hard by elements on both sides. The first group of opponents will be the friendly Muslim tyrants themselves, those regimes that stifle critiques from respected independent clerics and restrict their movements. The second group of opponents will come from the United States and will try to discredit the Muslim travelers by pointing to rash statements about Israel they may have made at one point or another. Given the passions aroused in the Middle East by the Arab-Israeli conflict, very few if any prominent Muslim figures will have the kind of liberal record of interfaith dialogue and tolerance that Americans find natural and appropriate. That should not disqualify them as potential interlocutors, however. Given the importance of the issues involved and the realities of the situation, the initial litmus test for being included in the conversation should be limited to a prohibition on incitement to terrorism and advocacy of war.

TURKISH DELIGHT?

AMERICANS NEED to be mindful of the extent to which Islam is entwined with politics throughout the Muslim world. This connection may pose problems, but it is a reality that cannot be changed by mere appeals for secularism. The United States should avoid the Manichean formulation adopted by Bush that nations are either "with us or with the terrorists"; that is not what is going on, any more than Islamism is what bin Laden calls "a struggle between Islam and unbelief." The real story is the potential rise of forces in the Muslim world that will change not Islam itself, but rather the human understanding of Islam, laying the groundwork for a Muslim Reformation and the eventual emergence of a politics at once authentically Islamist yet also authentically liberal and democratic. The encouragement of such trends should be an important objective of U.S. policy.

One successful model that merits emulation is Turkey. This is not because Turkey is "secular"; in fact, Turkish "secularism" is actually based on total state control and even repression of religion. Turkey is becoming a model precisely because Turkish democracy is beating back rigid state ideology and slowly and reluctantly permitting the emergence of Islamist movements and parties that reflect tradition, a large segment of public opinion, and the country's developing democratic spirit. Political Islam in Turkey has evolved rapidly out of an initially narrow and nondemocratic understanding of Islam into a relatively responsible force, whether it overlaps entirely with American ideals or not.

Other promising cases to explore include Kuwait, Bahrain, Morocco, Jordan, Yemen, Malaysia, and Indonesia—all of which are at differing stages of political and social liberalization and evolution. All are working to avoid the social explosion that comes with repression of Islamic politics as a vehicle of change. Opening the political process enables people to sort out the effective moderates from the rhetorical radicals and reactionaries. Significantly, citizens of these states have not been prominent among the major terrorist groups of the world, unlike citizens of the U.S. allies Egypt and Saudi Arabia.

Most great religions have elements of both tolerance and intolerance built into them: intolerance because they believe they carry the truth, perhaps the sole truth, and tolerance because they also speak of humanity, the common origins of mankind, concepts of divine justice, and a humane order for all. Violence does not flow from religion alone—even bigoted religion. After all, the greatest horrors and killing machines in history stemmed from the Western, secular ideologies of fascism and communism. Religion is not about to vanish from the face of the earth, even in the most advanced Western nations, and certainly not in the Islamic world. The West will have to deal with this reality and help open up these embittered societies. In the process, the multiple varieties of Islam—the key political realities of today—will either evolve in positive directions with popular support, or else be discredited when they deliver little but venom. Muslim publics will quickly know the difference when offered a choice.

Terrorists must be punished. But will Washington limit itself to a merely punitive agenda to treat only the symptoms of crisis in the Muslim world? A just settlement for the Palestinians and support of regional democratization remain among the key weapons that can fight the growth of terrorism. It will be a disaster for the United States, and another cruel chapter in the history of the Muslim world, if the war on terrorism fails to liberalize these battered societies and, instead, exacerbates those very conditions that contribute to the virulent anti-Americanism of today. If a society and its politics are violent and unhappy, its mode of religious expression is likely to be just the same.●

The Turmoil Within

The Struggle for the Future of the Islamic World

James Piscatori

What Went Wrong? Western Impact and Middle Eastern Response. BY BERNARD LEWIS. New York: Oxford University Press, 180 pp. $23.00.

Jihad: Expansion and Decline of the Islamist Movement. BY GILLES KEPEL. Cambridge: Belknap Press, 464 pp., $29.95.

LONG BEFORE the shattering events of September 11, two academic views—represented by Bernard Lewis and Gilles Kepel—had crystallized on the future of politicized Islam, or "Islamism." Lewis, a historian, argued that the movement's deep roots in Islamic history and thought guaranteed its potency and staying power; Kepel, a political sociologist, concluded that the Islamist moment had largely passed. Now two new books by these scholars, although mainly written before September, make it clear that recent events have not changed their contrary views.

In *What Went Wrong?*, Lewis' well-established argument that something has gone seriously awry with Islam has acquired new urgency. This prolific author draws on his profound knowledge of Middle Eastern and Islamic history to ask how a civilization that was once so materially successful and communally tolerant could have declined to the point where its economies are in free fall and political authoritarianism and violence have grown endemic. Where once great scientists, philosophers, and artists held sway,

---

JAMES PISCATORI is University Lecturer in Islamic Politics and Fellow at Wadham College, Oxford University, and author of *Muslim Politics*.

now thrive closed-minded didacts and "consecrated assassins." Lewis' history reveals an uneasy Muslim coexistence with unconquered infidels and an unwillingness to come to terms with the long-term dangers of fusing religion and politics.

Lewis' argument is nothing if not controversial. But he also defies some of his critics. He is more generous toward Islam than his detractors would acknowledge, for instance, seeing a greater indulgence in the medieval treatment of Muslim dissidents than was accorded supposed Christian heretics during the Spanish Inquisition. Moreover, contrary to the often-heard charge that he freezes Islamic history and fails to appreciate the extent of radical change in the twentieth century, Lewis is all too aware of powerful revisionist forces in Islam. These led, on the one hand, to Mustafa Kemal Atatürk's "secularizing" reforms in Turkey and, on the other, to Ayatollah Ruhollah Khomeini's Islamizing revolution in Iran.

The picture may be even more complex, however. As Kepel persuasively shows, the Turkey of today, with entrenched grassroots Islamic sentiment and an organized Islamist movement that can be repressed but not ignored, is scarcely what Atatürk envisioned. By the same token, the twists and turns of the Iranian Revolution have led, if not to the emergence of a fully operative civil society, then at least to portentous challenges to the monopoly of clerical rule in Iran. The Muslim world has not been isolated from the troublesome processes of modernization, class and ethnic differentiation, and the advent of mass education that, among other factors, have influenced the development of modern political societies throughout the world. New inequalities, identities, and opportunities have resulted.

More importantly, however, these social and political changes have also contributed to a fragmentation of religious authority whereby, to put it crudely, the meaning of scripture no longer needs to be interpreted by a religious establishment but, rather, lies in the eye of the beholder. Many Muslims would vehemently insist that the centuries-long development of Islamic jurisprudence and Koranic exegesis provides definitive guidance to the faithful. But this tradition now confronts the proliferation of modern-educated individuals, who have direct access to the basic religious texts and question why they should automatically defer to the religious class. It has thus become difficult to say with reassuring finality what is Islamic and what is not. This shifting of goal posts and the ease with which individuals can presume to invoke and defend Muslim tradition have allowed Osama bin Laden to claim to speak on behalf of Islam. Radicalization, therefore, appears to have emerged as much from distinctly modern conditions as from the prior experience of inauspicious Muslim-Western encounters.

RUMBLES IN THE REALM

LEWIS CANNOT BE ACCUSED of taking his subjects lightly. On the contrary, by urging Muslims to ask themselves what they have done wrong, he seeks to rouse them from passive and self-defeating victimhood—"the West has done this to us"—to an active and honest re-examination of their predicament that would locate the problem closer to home. First incurious of the distant West, then pointing an accusatory finger at the imperialist West, Muslims, through their insularity, have done themselves a singular disservice. They have fallen prey to "predatory authority" in their own societies: governments that, in the name of modernization or Islam (or both), intimidate their people in order to maintain their narrow rule.

If Muslims are being asked to take destiny into their own hands, however, the consequences will not be entirely what was anticipated. Many Muslims, in fact, have already been asking just the question Lewis poses to them. Terrorists and radicals have not answered it in the way he would like, of course, nor have they evinced the faltering cultural self-confidence that he suggests is a hallmark of the Muslim modern age. On the contrary, Islamist extremists unflinchingly seek to return to what the Koran calls the "straight path" of Islam through overthrow of their rulers, whom they consider impious, as well as confrontation with outsiders, whom they regard as infidels. From bin Laden's perspective, states such as Saudi Arabia or Pakistan may proclaim themselves to be Islamic but are actually "allies of Satan."

But other Muslim voices offer a different prescription for their societies' ills. Muslim reformers are formulating—tentatively and, thus far, inconclusively—a Muslim position on pluralism and political participation. Some may automatically assume that these reformers would eventually replace what Lewis calls one "shabby" tyranny with another, but noteworthy are the groups advocating for women, human rights, and other special interests that are increasingly making their views known and heard. Many Muslims now argue that Islam and democracy are indeed compatible—taking the debate away from those who consider democracy an alien system at variance with obedience to divine rather than popular sovereignty and a complete, revealed law that makes a legislative body superfluous. An increasing number of Muslim intellectuals in societies as diverse as Egypt, Jordan, Iran, Turkey, Indonesia, and Malaysia are now concerned with how what they regard as the intrinsically Islamic values of pluralism, tolerance, and civic participation can be implemented.

Taken together, these agents of radical and moderate opinion give us a picture of roiling Muslim societies, preoccupied with their own unfaithfulness or inefficiency and uncertain how to reconcile the contradictory prescriptions, but in some cases intent on creating an Islamic state or Islamizing their societies. With the images of the destruction at the World Trade Center and the Pentagon freshly in mind, we may be forgiven for failing to see the full complexities of the internal Islamic situation. As Lewis elegantly explains, intercivilizational contacts have often been difficult. Yet to view the intricate problems and prospects of modern Muslims through the framework of a clash between Islam and the West (or even more generally of East versus West), as *What Went Wrong?* occasionally does, is to become preoccupied with a balance sheet that tells, at best, only part of today's story. "Imbalance" and "painful asymmetry" may well have characterized the Muslim-Western relationship since the seventeenth century. But there has also been a turning inward by Muslims that challenges the status quo—political, economic, social, gendered. And these challenges lie beyond and, in many ways, take precedence over relations with any outside world.

Moreover, the Islamic realm is itself in the process of redefinition as Muslim minorities become a permanent and indigenous presence in the Western societies of Europe, North America, and Australia. And these Muslim minorities, who live with the daily demands of an open society, are especially important to the work of the reformers in shifting the terms of the debate away from the radicals.

WHITHER JIHAD?

SHOULD WE CONCLUDE that the Islamist challenge, or what some refer to as the Islamist revolt, is bound to fail? Prior to September 11, Kepel and others, notably Olivier Roy in *The Failure of Political Islam*, argued that a combination of state power and Islamist intellectual incoherence was fatally wounding Islamist movements before they could bring their vision to fruition. A prime example is post-1979 Iran, where the policy of exporting the revolution dismally failed and a domestic "clerisocracy," to use the word coined by the late political scientist P. J. Vatikiotis, has remained on top of a fairly secular society through sheer authoritarianism, not moral worthiness.

Kepel's *Jihad* builds on an impressively extensive investigation of Islamist movements across the world to document this relative decline in their effect and appeal. Like Lewis, Kepel constructs an expansive and forceful argument but keeps his eyes on events since the late 1960s. Setting out to chart the rise and fall of a utopian movement, Kepel capably points to the combination of actors that provided both its strength and its ultimate weakness. The discontents unleashed by the modernizing, nationalist regimes of the 1950s and 1960s mobilized the urban young, elements of the middle classes—the pious bourgeois of the *suqs* (bazaars) and the professionals—and Islamist intellectuals. With all the certainty that a vaguely defined but symbolically charged religious agenda can provide, these Muslim visionaries grew in influence and number throughout the 1970s. The Iranian Revolution, however, sharpened intra-Muslim conflict and raised the question of whether the Iranian regime or the Saudi monarchy should lead the Islamic cause. The subsequent decade seemed to settle the matter, however: the Iran-Iraq War diverted and sapped Iranian power while the Afghan jihad against the Soviet Union cast Saudi Arabia and Pakistan into the role of defenders of the *umma* (pan-Islamic community). The conservative forces became dominant.

In the 1990s, the situation changed again, but the trend of radical Islamist decline continued. The introduction of U.S. forces into Saudi Arabia split the Islamist base; the urban poor and radical intellectuals vehemently opposed the Saudis now, whereas the middle class was torn but conscious of the side on which its bread was buttered. Into this gap stepped the state—whether Egyptian, Saudi, Turkish, Algerian, Tunisian, or other—deliberately seeking to split the movement further, co-opting those it could and repressing those it could not. Suicide bombings, hostage-taking, and other terrorist actions continued, but (actions against Israel aside) they increasingly seemed acts of desperation. By the end of the century, the signs of jihad's failure seemed everywhere.

Broadly persuasive as it is, Kepel's analysis comes up hard against turn-of-the-century events. The Taliban were certainly "puffed up" by Pakistan and the United States, as he says, but the life they acquired in league with bin Laden's al Qaeda network suggests something other than a collapse under the weight of their own contradictions. As we know, it took the United States and its allies to bring down the Taliban's so-called Islamic emirate, and some of the Taliban's ideas about a politicized Islam are bound to live on. Still, attacks such as those of September 11, in Kepel's view, are a rapidly depreciating resource, destined to backfire and increasingly isolate the radicals.

This is a utilitarian account—states using movements, movements using hapless members, strategies that in the end reflect a tactical, radical Islamism beyond its sell-by date. As much truth as there is in these observations, they give only a partial picture. And Lewis' study provides the cautionary complement: mindless violence has roots in politicized versions of history that carry social weight of their own. The implication to draw from Lewis' account is that it is not the history presented by eminent historians that counts. Rather, as historian R. Stephen Humphreys points out in

Memory and Desire: The Middle East in a Troubled Age, it is the local memory, how Muslim ideologues package and present history, that is galvanizing.

KEEPING THE FAITH

WHETHER WE REGARD BIN LADEN as the final cry of a whimpering revolution or as a disconcertingly representative voice for the future, Kepel's *Jihad* is compelling in identifying another important trend. The radicals may have come unstuck, he argues, but the moderates have not. Here he goes beyond what Lewis would allow and finds the struggle for integrating democratic ideas with Muslim values a defining aspect of modern Muslim experience. Yet it is not entirely clear whom he means by the "democrats."

The problem is partly one of terminology: Is there such a thing as a moderate Islamist? At times Kepel seems to suggest the answer is no, straightforwardly equating Islamism with radicalism. Yet he also refers to a particular kind of belief—"radical," "militant," or "jihadist" Islamism—thereby, more usefully, implying a range of opinion within the category. If valid, this more expansive characterization implies that evolution of thought is possible among those Muslims who are expressly committed to political action. Moreover, it colors our view of what exactly is supposed to be in decline.

There are several ways of looking at this. One way is to assume that ideological rigidity or perhaps incoherence renders Islamism incapable of real development; it is, therefore, destined to fail. Another possibility, however, is that the very ambiguity of Islamist thought, in addition to providing the practical advantage of attracting a broad constituency, allows space for the flexible development of talismanic ideas such as the "Islamic state." If this view is taken, then, far from being destined to decline, Islamism is capable of adaptation and growth. Indeed, Kepel's own analysis points to an "equivocal" set of ideas that just might evolve into a "Muslim form of democracy." This hybrid would be true to its heritage but would also be the modern, pragmatic product of a series of compromises and conflicts with regimes reluctant, but impelled, to share power.

In this sense, then, Islamism may have a future, even if militancy, in Kepel's optimistic view, does not make long-term sense.

What is clear, at least, is that Kepel does not mean to endorse the secular solution to the Muslim political quandary. Yet other observers of Islam have invested much faith in its healing powers, and its attraction has only grown in the past eight months. Lewis speaks tantalizingly of a "Christian remedy" to Muslim (and Jewish) ills—that is, separation of religious and political functions. Salman Rushdie can be forgiven for having a definite view on the subject. In the British *Guardian* newspaper, he lamented the rise of tit-for-tat communal murders in India but pointed to a larger perspective: "Something we don't want to look at in the face: namely, that in India, as elsewhere in our darkening world, religion is the poison in the blood. ... What happened in India happened in God's name. The problem's name is God." For the overwhelming majority of Muslims, however, this view is neither theologically nor culturally acceptable. Many would object that it makes little political sense as well. For them, Turkey's putative secularism has been nothing more than the subjugation of religious institutions to the overweening power of the state.

A politically charged Islam, which automatically rejects the secular option, does not necessarily have to degenerate into the obscurantist beliefs, priestly tyrannies, and sacred violence that secular ideologues anticipate. Yet there is no guarantee that these pitfalls will be avoided, or that radicalism's force is spent. Muslim societies are in uncertain transition, and internal preoccupations are arguably more significant in the long run than anti-Westernism. Neither Lewis' Islamist "rage and self-pity" nor Kepel's "trail of decline" seems inevitable. The struggle over who speaks for Islam is far from over.⊛